Roaring Reptiles, Bountiful Citrus, and Neon Pies

UNIVERSITY PRESS OF FLORIDA

Florida A&M University, Tallahassee
Florida Atlantic University, Boca Raton
Florida Gulf Coast University, Ft. Myers
Florida International University, Miami
Florida State University, Tallahassee
New College of Florida, Sarasota
University of Central Florida, Orlando
University of Florida, Gainesville
University of North Florida, Jacksonville
University of South Florida, Tampa
University of West Florida, Pensacola

University Press of Florida
Gainesville · Tallahassee · Tampa · Boca Raton
Pensacola · Orlando · Miami · Jacksonville · Ft. Myers · Sarasota

Roaring REPTILES, *Bountiful* CITRUS, *and* NEON PIES

An Unofficial Guide to Florida's Official Symbols

Mark Lane

24 23 22 21 20 19   6 5 4 3 2 1

Illustrations by Erica Group Kiel

ISBN 978-0-8130-6623-3
Library of Congress Control Number: 2019939490

The University Press of Florida is the scholarly publishing agency for the State University System of Florida, comprising Florida A&M University, Florida Atlantic University, Florida Gulf Coast University, Florida International University, Florida State University, New College of Florida, University of Central Florida, University of Florida, University of North Florida, University of South Florida, and University of West Florida.

University Press of Florida
2046 NE Waldo Road
Suite 2100
Gainesville, FL 32609
http://upress.ufl.edu

In Memory of June Lane

Contents

Helpful Letter to School Librarians

It's come to my attention that a few of you—the ones who still have the budget for buying books—may purchase this work by mistake. Hey, it's a book about our great state's symbols with history doled out in easy doses. What better way to teach your young charges about how lucky they are to live in a state represented by mockingbirds, Key lime pies, and dangerous reptiles!

Sadly, this is not that book. It's full of the kind of unnecessary commentary that might cause trouble. Some will accuse this book of disrespect toward our state's most revered symbols. That it mocks the mockingbird. Ridicules the antebellum origins of our state pie. Questions the awesomeness of our never-performed state play. That it celebrates our glorious ancestors as no more than schmoes like us only in better costumes. That it paints the very act of legislating on state symbols as the result of political calculations that are at best silly and at worst tawdry. Not the sort of things young leaders of tomorrow need to read.

As you know, it only takes one ticked-off parent and before you know it, the school board, local newspaper, American

Civil Liberties Union, and online superpatriots are involved. Soon people with matching T-shirts are filing into the seats at school board meetings. Soon the legislature will modify the social studies standards again. And soon everyone will be faced with new standardized tests and mandated courses because that's how Florida responds to educational controversies. Nobody wants that.

And you thought you were buying a simple state symbols roundup. My apologies. Unfortunately, the purchase price is nonrefundable if you've already pasted a Dewey decimal sticker on the spine. Sorry, I don't make the rules.

My suggestion is to write in an "R" on that sticker, put it on the reference shelf, and sit back secure in the knowledge that no young person will discover it there. Then, as a bonus, it also will be available for your guilty enjoyment anytime you want.

—*The author*

Preface

WHEN THE FLORIDA LEGISLATURE is in session, it's always worthwhile to watch the movements between the House and Senate chambers from a roost on the fifth floor: you'll see the lobbyists buzzing about lobbying, aides out aiding, administrative assistants assisting, and reporters reporting. You might notice that the oval opening between floors is decorated with a list of the official state this and the official state that.

Whenever I'm there, I idly run down the list while taking in the atmosphere: April 2, State Day; In God We Trust, State Motto; Sunshine State, State Nickname; Orange Blossom, State Flower; and Key Lime, State Pie. Florida loves official state designations. The rotunda listings, although numerous, are but a partial menu. Like authorizing specialty license plates, declaring official state objects, creatures, holidays, and works of art is a legislative exercise that's hard to stop once you get going.

Each one is a cheap way to make somebody happy, and what politician doesn't enjoy that? Still, these decisions can carry unsuspected baggage. And because Florida is a state with a fluid identity, deciding the things that represent us at any given moment is far trickier than it appears on the surface. Even in a place trying to be a democratic republic, branding is not for amateurs.

"If you were a tree, what kind of tree would you be?" as Barbara Walters famously asked on the air in 1981. If you were a Florida legislator in 1953, that would be easy. We'd be a sabal palm. They're everywhere. You see one and feel at home. Okay, what kind of bird are we? A more sensitive question. There are political and economic ramifications. What kind of marine mammal are we? And if the manatee is truly our state's spirit-animal, why is everyone okay with letting boats run over them all the time? This whole business gets complicated fast.

Florida is a place that changes identity in a hurry. In a pinch, we'll dress up in borrowed clothes and try out somebody else's identity. We're the Old South. No, we're the Bright American Sunbelt High Tech Future. No, we're just like the rest of the nation. No, we're proud exotics. Since a lot of us are from someplace else—U.S. Census Bureau figures find only Arizona has a smaller percentage of native-born residents—we shamelessly import.

Just look at the pediment of the grand old Florida Capitol in Tallahassee. There's a scene that meant to embody our mythology. You'll see a cigar-store Indian, an improbably built steamship, and mountains. Ah, the Florida Mountains. The scene is from the official state seal, but you'd think somewhere along the line somebody might have noticed that before they started building the place.

That old capitol building stands in front of the new capitol building as a warning to any legislator who thinks state symbolism is a job that won't get superseded. And maybe this has proved instructive because each legislative session I scan the House and Senate calendars for new efforts to divine our state identity with new animals, plants, objects, or works of art, and I'm saddened that these efforts have lately slacked off despite the recent additions of official state horse and state cattle breeds. (The cracker horse and cracker cattle.) I see this a symptom of a decline in civic spirit. Maybe legislators are looking up at the rotunda listings and figuring there's no room. Nonsense! There's always room for more.

People make fun of the legislature for wasting time on this enterprise. This is misguided. There are far worse things lawmakers could be doing with their time—as they prove every year. Fixing our identity on inanimate objects and animal life that gets no say in the matter is the kind of group decision that people started doing as soon as they formed into primitive societies. These totems and mascots are our attempts to pin down who we are, to make visible previously vague feelings of common identity. When legislators get it wrong it's because they've misunderstood the people around them and often themselves. Which is instructive too. It's why the official state freshwater fish (Florida largemouth bass) matters. We are the Bass People. At least in inland Florida. Myself, I live among the Manatee People on the coast.

Florida is a confederation of regions and tribes, which is another thing that makes this work difficult. We resist unifying efforts. Always have. Which is why Floridians like strong political leaders; it's no fun getting in the way of weak ones.

The following is by no means a complete listing of the official state this or that. I didn't have the heart to go to the official state Renaissance festival. That the official state flagship (the schooner *Western Union*) is taking water, suffering from wood rot and lack of repair funding, is too painfully symbolic to delve into. I cherry-picked a few high points. Perhaps this exercise might prove a useful guide for future state-sponsored investigations into Florida's cultural identity. A warning to elementary school classes that are often tempted to take this on: if the various spirit-animals and regional totems we honor tell us anything, it's that identity is a shifting thing and always ready for revision.

Roaring Reptiles, Bountiful Citrus, and Neon Pies

OFFICIAL STATE PIE

Key Lime

Key Lime Pie

Pie Wedge or Candy-Colored Wedge Issue?

Key lime pie is designated as the official Florida state pie.
—Florida Statute 15.052

Key lime pies are the pink flamingos of Florida food.
—Sen. Larcenia Bullard

It's all there. A lot of contradictions baked into a pie. Which is why Key lime pie is the ideal Florida state pie and the best official state pastry in the nation.

A Key lime pie mixes the natural (eggs, limes) and the manufactured (kryptonite-green dye in inauthentic versions, sweetened condensed milk in all versions). The exotic (hard-to-find Key limes) and the mundane (eggs, graham crackers). The tart and the sweet. The cracker (graham) and the tropical (limes).

It's a homemade pie that usually requires the output from two separate factories: a condensed milk factory and a place that bottles Key lime or other limes made from concentrate, because really, for a convenience dessert, who goes out seeking and squeezing Key limes, Persian limes, or the other substitutes for the elusive *Citrus aurantifolia*? No, make that three factories: also a pie crust from Publix because that's how mama used to make it.

Most of the ingredients come from somewhere else—the limes are usually from Mexican groves—but all are whipped together here, so it counts as a local delicacy. It can look garish when tarted up with food coloring and poufy whipped cream topping. Or it can look bland, a faded wallpaper yellow on the outside hiding the rich pleasures within.

And its rise and national acceptance make it a symbol for big shifts in state power and tastes. Proof of how Florida power and population shifted from rural north Florida to urban southern Florida, from inland to coastal. Which is why it took repeated tries to nudge the Florida Legislature into bestowing official state symbol status upon the pie in 2006. Yes, that late. The pie ran up against hard-shell political power wielded by North Florida legislators on behalf of pecan pie, a delicacy of the Old South that straddles the gooey line between pie and candy bar.

The first try came in 1988 by South Florida Democrat Rep. Norman "Norm" Ostrau and Key West Democrat Rep. Ron Saunders. Although the measure passed the House, it was ignored in the tradition-bound Senate, where Dempsey Barron, Senate dean and loud voice for all things North Florida, pronounced sweet potato pie just plain better and everybody knows it. And who in that body would oppose views of the powerful Rules Committee chairman on matters of dessert?

In 1994, when State Rep. Debbie Wasserman Schultz—from down south in Broward County, naturally—sponsored a Key lime pie measure in the Florida House, she had to settle for half a slice: a resolution declaring the pie to be an "important symbol of Florida." An important symbol, was that the best they could come up with?

Too little, too late. But the lines were drawn for a recurring pie fight, one that pitted North Florida against South Florida. Interstate 10 against State Road A1A. Calhoun County against Broward County. Nuts against fruits. Earth tones against pastels. Country cookin' against resort cuisine.

"Key lime pies are the pink flamingos of Florida food," declared State Sen. Larcenia Bullard of Miami, as she championed the state pie measure in 2006. True words but baffling to many north of the Pink Flamingo Belt. (After her death, the U.S. House of Representatives resolution honoring her listed her state pie effort among her achievements.)

But North Florida interests still fought back hard. A pecan grower from Live Oak, State Rep. Dwight Stansel, argued against the measure. As a last-ditch maneuver, he filed a substitute amendment favoring sweet potato pie, noting that sweet potatoes are a valuable crop in Florida, while a lot of those pie limes were alien citrus crossing in from the border with Mexico. But by dessert time, the Florida House vote was 106–14 in favor of Key lime as the state pie.

Stansel later told the *Miami Herald* he was only kidding in his opposition. Actually, "just cuttin' the fool," was the story's money quote. "Make it chicken pot pie," he said. "We got too many damn things to worry about besides pie." Sour lime sentiments.

In the analysis prepared by legislative staff before the votes, researchers declared that the proposed legislation raised no constitutional questions and had no budgetary impact. "Currently, no pie is designated as the official state pie," the report correctly noted, so there was no conflict with existing law.

But then researchers made another claim for the pie, a curious one. "The first Key lime pie was created in the 1850s in South Florida." In this oft-heard claim, pie supporters went a bite too far.

The general excellence of Key lime pie in all its forms—even the versions with cornstarch, tapioca, glycerin or cream cheese inside and with nondairy whipped cream from a pressurized can on top, or frozen on a stick—cannot be gainsaid. But like much of Florida life, it was a twentieth-century invention, an improvisation to deal with local conditions. It doesn't have an old-timey tradition.

The earliest printed cookbook references to the pie are from the 1940s. If it existed before then, nobody said so in print. I cannot guess where the 1850s date came from except that it has been dutifully passed along by cookbook writers, lifestyle feature writers, and menu-blurb writers over the years. But it's unlikely for the simple reason that the pie's key ingredient is sweetened condensed milk, a product that was not patented by Gail Borden Jr. until 1856.

Borden organized his company in 1857, and after several false starts didn't get things on a full-scale production basis until the 1860s, just in time to supply a federal government with armies to feed. As a popular consumer product, the cans of milk would still take a few decades to turn into a familiar, nationally available, found-on-any-store-shelf commodity.

But one of Florida's oldest tourism traditions is laying claim to much older, more venerable and colorful history than anything that jibes with what we laughingly call reality. Living in a place that was sparsely settled before World War

II, Floridians sometimes long for more southern history than we actually possess—although not enough to cause trouble. We want the ante without the bellum.

Which is why we build stately columns at the entrances of subdivisions and castle turrets out of cinderblock and rebar. We name our streets and towns as though they are from lost civilizations from Castile to Gondor. We hold Civil War re-enactments on the soccer field behind the 7-Eleven. And we claim our official state pie predates factories that turned out its main ingredient on any scale.

Some articles and cookbooks flesh out this claim by giving credit to one Aunt Sally, cook for William Curry (1821–1896), a wealthy Key West salvager and businessman. But instead of being a gift from the kitchen of the richest man in town, a top-down recipe, Key lime pie is more likely a bottom-up, Depression Era recipe. As befits our state pie.

In its early years the pie might have seemed more pre-fab than the quality folks would go for. Instead, it was a humble pie. One that became local color and worked its way up the menu. From home to roadside snack shack, to diner, to hotel restaurant, to clip 'n' save magazine recipe. An adaptation to harsh local conditions that caught on and went national.

Getting milk in the Keys was always a problem. In 1939 *The WPA Guide to Florida* warned Key West travelers: "Since the island furnishes little forage for cows and supports but one dairy and a flock of goats, evaporated milk is usually served." (It mentions Key limes too but, tellingly, is silent on the pie question.)

Meanwhile, the Borden Company had been turning out pamphlets, cookbooks, and ads with pie recipes using its sweetened condensed milk. A recipe printed just after World

War I, in the pamphlet *Borden's Evaporated Milk Book of Recipes,* has a lemon meringue pie recipe that looks like our beloved pie. (Sadly, it needed cornstarch so that it would set, like some of the Key-lime-pies-in-name-only that one still sees trotted out to a credulous public.) By the mid-1930s Borden promoted a "Magic Lemon Meringue Pie" recipe that was just like our state pie, only lemony.

It was but a matter of time before somebody would throw the local lime into the commercial recipe, and wow, it worked. It worked even better than lemons because Key limes are more acidic and can firm up a filling without help.

By 1940 Monroe Boston Strause—popularly dubbed "the pie king," the inventor of chiffon pie and an all-around celebrity chef before his time—wrote instructions in a commercial kitchen trade magazine for making Key lime pies six at a time. "No sooner was the rumor about that I was on the trail of the best Key lime pie formula in Florida than invitations came pouring in like a tropical cloudburst for me to come on over and sample the finest Key Lime Pie in the South," he wrote. He settled on a Miami restaurant version of this "very popular pie in Florida."

By 1948 a Key lime pie recipe found its way into *A Date with a Dish: A Cook Book of American Negro Recipes*—oddly, not from Florida but from a Detroit-based chef. Yes, it used regular old lime juice but still called the result Key lime pie. Purists no doubt shuddered.

The next year the Key West Women's Club published its *Key West Cook Book,* a cleverly illustrated, written-out-in-cursive, spiral-bound cookbook that is a founding document of Florida cooking. It exudes the spirit of the place: funky, uneven, idiosyncratic, eclectic, and humorous. (Mmmm, turtle steak, but be sure to cut it thin and pound it with plate's edge to tenderize.)

And there on page 215 is the familiar three-ingredient Key lime pie. Use whatever pie shell you want. "Bake in a slow oven until brown." No times or temperatures mentioned. In our microwavable age, I like that phrase, "a slow oven." Anything oven-made feels slow to me.

The Key West Women's Club recipe appeared to be the instruction sheet for putting the pie on the national dessert shelf. After that the pie shows up everywhere. That same year a version of the pie smothered with a meringue thick enough for silent-movie slapstick appeared in the *Miami Herald* with the headline declaration: "Key lime pie is popular Florida fare."

Like South Florida itself, sometime around the end of World War II the pie went mainstream. It went from being mentioned strictly as local color in travel features (the earliest mention in the *New York Times* was in a 1940 travel column) to the food page. The pie had been mentioned along with turtle steak as equally exotic culinary local color in a 1951 *Life* photo feature about the press corps enjoying President Harry Truman's Key West vacation.

By the 1950s even Florida newspaper recipes advised adding the much-reviled green food coloring. It "gives the custard an inviting appearance," advised the *St. Petersburg Times* in 1952. One shudders. But tourists expected to see tropical pastels, and houseguests wanted to reproduce what they had seen back at the hotel restaurant. It took decades for pie traditionalists to educate Floridians and tourists otherwise. That the state pie statute fails to specify the yellow version of the pie is a clear legislative oversight.

Folklorist and activist Stetson Kennedy was among those who registered disgust. "With very, very few exceptions, none of the pies being served by that name have ever seen a real Key lime," he wrote. "By and large they are a concoction of tapioca (or whatever it is that store-bought pies are made of), some sugar green coloring, and citric acid, or at best a little juice from a Perrine lime or Persian lime."

The local Key limes, all but wiped out in hurricanes of the 1920s and 1930s, became hard to find in the Keys. By 1965 State Rep. Bernie Papy Jr., a second-generation Keys legislator, was so revolted at the stuff passing itself off as Key lime pie that he and some citrus-belt representatives sponsored a bill making it "unlawful to use the term 'Key lime' in advertisement for any food preparation or product unless the preparation or product contains the actual fruit or extract of the 'Key lime.'" Those selling regular old lime pies as Key lime pies could be fined $100. The bill went to the agriculture committee, whence it was never heard of again. Nonetheless, point made.

By 1983 the pie was so mainstream, so part of the repertoire of any knowledgeable cook anywhere in the country that it was the weapon of choice for cookbook writer Rachel Samstat when her philandering husband required a pie in the face in Nora Ephron's novel *Heartburn*. A perfect choice: less of a cliché than a cream pie; more tart than a chiffon pie; less risk of permanent clothing and property damage than a blueberry pie: a considerate, sophisticated, thinking woman's pie in the face.

Thirty years earlier, this choice would have required some explanation and backstory. Samstat was from New York, not Florida. But by 1975 Key lime pie instructions were in the *Joy of Cooking,* and so in the 1980s the pie would easily be in the arsenal of any maritally wronged cook. Heck, it was in the frozen food aisle for anyone pressed for time while arming herself.

The novel helpfully includes a recipe. Samstat is not the kind of cookbook writer who demands Key limes of her readers. Lime juice of any kind is fine. "Even bottled lime juice will do," she assures us. Cookbooks say that a lot. It is wrong.

Can this be a true Florida dish without Ping-Pong ball–sized limes from Mexico? Hurricane Andrew finished off the remnants of commercial Key lime production in South Florida, which means the Keys part of the equation is no more than an origin story now that the pie has gone international and evolved into hundreds of variations. Still, the pie requires that exact fruit or call it something else.

Perhaps the drafters of the Key lime pie statute were wise to leave out any specific language defining what they meant when they talked about Key lime pie. Florida Statute 15.052 is but one sentence long: "Key lime pie is designated as the official Florida state pie." So whatever you choose to call Key lime pie—yellow or green, eggless or egged, barely cooked or safely baked, with or without Key limes, with or without meringue, with a store-bought crust, something with vanilla wafers or whole grains, or even something picked up whole out of the frozen dessert case—it's all officially ours.

This is Florida. We'll run with the general concept and tell the tourists that's how Aunt Sally made it. And where did she get the ingredients? Who knows? Maybe when she was captured by pirates. Pirates carrying limes so sour they could only be used for boat drinks. And they demanded she whip up a dessert or walk the plank. At wits' end, she found a recipe on the back of a can of condensed milk and improvised. As the buccaneers dozed off in a carbohydrate-induced stupor, she made her escape, swimming to Key West and fighting off sharks with a can opener until rescued by a kindly Key West salvage boat crew, friendly natives, or kids on Spring Break. The rest is history, at least the kind we heard on the tour bus.

○

Kermit's Key lime pie

Here is a Key lime pie recipe courtesy of Kermit's Key West Key Lime Shoppe. They assure me their juice is made from actual Key limes, just not Key limes from Florida because those aren't available commercially. It is bottled in DeLand, however, so it can boast a Florida origin.

INGREDIENTS:

A 9-inch graham cracker crust
Two 14-ounce cans of sweetened condensed milk
Six egg yolks
Half-cup Key lime juice

DIRECTIONS:

Blend milk and eggs at a low speed until smooth. Add Key lime juice and finish blending. Pour into the pie crust and bake in a preheated 300-degree F oven for 15 minutes. Cool for 15 minutes before refrigerating. Serve cold, topped with fresh whipped cream.

Important note: This recipe uses Kermit's Key lime juice, which is double strength. For Key lime juices that aren't that strong, or if you're making your own Key lime juice (which is messy and tedious and the seeds will be everywhere, but hats off to you if you do), use one cup of Key lime juice.

Unimportant note: Don't you dare reach for green food coloring unless you're being ironic. Myself, I don't believe in putting any topping on the pie because that detracts attention from the pie itself, the pie *qua* pie, which needs no further help. I have been known, however, to add Key lime zests to fancy things up. Leftover peels can be used in gin and tonics after and during baking, because you deserve it.

OFFICIAL STATE NICKNAME

Sunshine State

Slogan

Welcome to the Sunshine— Not the Alligator—State

Section 1. The term "Sunshine State" is hereby designated as the official nickname of the State of Florida.

—House Concurrent Resolution 5514 (1970)

I HAVE THIS FASCINATION with civic slogans. The cornier, the stranger, the better. This comes in part from workaday newspaper writing, where it's perfectly normal to use some bizarre slogan on second reference as a place-name substitute. And because here in the Sunshine State I grew up in the World's Most Famous Beach, which everyone knows is Daytona Beach.

I love my hometown slogan because it's an obvious, upfront lie about how my little town actually is kind of a big deal. This disconnect from reality gives it the feel of a local joke. When you say it, people wonder if you're putting them on. And you probably are. Putting on the tourists is a rich Florida tradition.

The city slogan's origins date to sometime in the 1910s, and it was cemented in place during a few weeks of excellent publicity in 1930s when daredevil drivers set land-speed records on our hard-packed sands, witnessed by the world's sporting press, celebrities, and newsreel cameramen.

In our modern branding environment a slogan like that sounds like a parody of old-time Florida tourism boosterism. It makes the sophisticated marketing professional cringe; something else in its favor.

I suspect our beloved state slogan "the Sunshine State" also makes the sophisticated marketer cringe. To be precise, it's our official state nickname, as belatedly recognized by the legislature in 1970. Like my town's nickname, we didn't claim it first—we swiped it in front of everyone, but it's still beloved.

The Sunshine State slogan has been a feature on our license plates since 1949. That date is significant. Before World War II Florida was known by all kinds of sobriquets— the Peninsula State, the Everglades State, the Alligator State . . . nothing stuck in the popular imagination. Highlighting your biggest swamp or scariest reptile is not always the best pitch for moving real estate or attracting tourists.

"Florida is called the Alligator State because its creeks and rivers and swamps are full of alligators," *The Rainbow Book of American Folk Tales and Legends* still cheerfully explained to children in the 1950s. Let's go there, Daddy! Will there be bears, too? And sharks? What about pythons? And we'll get to see them? Promise?

After World War II, as road systems expanded and mass-market tourism exploded, Florida took on the sunshine state slogan already used by California, New Mexico, and South Dakota. South Dakota even had the slogan stitched to its flag. No matter. Sunshine became our state identity, one we claim in the face of summers full of 2:00 p.m. Old Testament–style thunderstorms and active hurricane seasons. "Florida, folks: Land of perpetual sunshine. Let's get the auction started before we have a tornado," Groucho Marx announced before unloading swampland on the rubes in the 1929 movie *The Cocoanuts.* Our dramatic weather was already a national joke at the dawn of the talkies.

The Sunshine State name seldom appeared in print until the Great Land Boom of the 1920s that was parodied in that movie. But Land Boom sales forces made such vigorous use of the phrase that by the 1930s it felt like a permanent part of the promotional landscape. "Florida has always been called the Sunshine state," Carita Doggett firmly asserted in the Depression Era book she produced for the Florida State Hotel Commission, *Florida: Empire of the Sun,* without fear of contradiction.

The Sunshine State license plate bill seemed overdue by the time it was introduced by State Sen. Joseph Johnston of Brooksville in 1949. Johnston served only one term in the Florida Legislature as part of a rich and varied professional career, but when he died in 2009, the headline in the *St. Petersburg Times* read, "Epilogue: Joseph Johnston, father of Sunshine State license plate."

And that is what he was remembered for: putting the state nickname on every Florida road and parking lot and imprinting the phrase into the Florida consciousness. Soon the nickname Alligator State crawled into the swamp of historical memory.

Florida's success at heisting the slogan was so complete that by 1992 South Dakota gave up and redesigned its flag. There was no use in even trying anymore. They hauled down their flag, surrendering in the face of the raw marketing power of Florida tourism.

As somebody born well after 1949, I have the Sunshine State identity stamped onto my consciousness. I have no memory of hearing my home called anything else. I've driven the Sunshine State Parkway, drilled my kids so they'd meet the Sunshine State Standards set by the Department of Education, and cheered for Embry-Riddle Aeronautical University's teams playing in the Sunshine State Conference; I've written extensively in defense of the government in the Sunshine Law and can sing "Come to the Florida Sunshine Tree" from memory. The sunshine thing, symbolized by the smiling sun wearing shades on every tourism map and state attractions postcard, is inescapable.

The Sunshine State is Florida's identity reduced to one of the ancients' four elements: We are fire. It is our economy reduced to one draw: We are for tourists. And it encapsulates the single best comeback we have when people complain about things here: Yeah sure, but it's bright outside most of the time. Can't argue with that. Yes, we are also a bright spot for crime, drugs, poor mental hygiene, political craziness, state and municipal corruption, heedless driving, poorly maintained infrastructure, underfunded schools, environmental destruction, sinkholes, lightning, hurricanes, sharks, and pythons, and sure, sea-level rise may cause the entire coastal enterprise to slide into the sea like Atlantis— but damn, it's nice and bright outside. Even in February.

We're not the Mental Health State. We're the Sunshine State. Come on down!

OFFICIAL STATE REPTILE

Alligator

Reptile

The Fiercest State Symbol in the Whole Swamp

The American alligator is hereby designated and declared
as the official Florida state reptile.

—Florida Statute 15.0385

ALLIGATORS ARE DANGEROUS CREATURES for Florida writers. They lure well-intentioned observers into a swamp of vivid regional stereotyping and exaggerated danger.

I'm guilty. So are most journalists. So are travel writers, mystery writers, and airboat passengers who post on social media. As a Florida newspaper reporter, I am aware that any story with an alligator in it, even as a walk-on extra, has a built-in audience. They are cold-blooded click magnets. Especially when they are part of a crime story. The stereotypical Florida Man arrest story should involve (1) an alligator and (2) drugs or alcohol, with bonus points for sex, nudity, misguided videography, and do-it-yourself projects gone horribly awry. Example headline from a 2018 story that went viral from the *Bradenton Herald:* "'Y'all got beer still?' Florida Man Runs Around Store Chasing Customer with Live Alligator."

Almost perfect. "He Was Naked, on Crack, and in Alligator's Mouth—Florida Man's Ordeal" (*Seattle Times* headline; *Orlando Sentinel* story). Perfect.

This is a trend from the dawn of Florida travel lit. Consider when naturalist and explorer William Bartram encountered the "the subtle, greedy alligator" in 1774, near present-day Legoland:

> Behold him rushing forth from the flags and reeds. His enormous body swells. His plaited tail brandished high, floats upon the lake. The waters like a cataract descend from his opening jaws. Clouds of smoke issue from his dilated nostrils. The earth trembles with his thunder.

Yup, smoke from the nostrils, a real-life dragon. The beasts bring this out in writers.

As they should. They let us know that here is a place rich in casual danger, the kind you don't need to dress up for. A primal swamp red in tooth and claw lying in wait on the edge of what appears to be a paradise only on the surface.

I get a warm feeling when tourists stop me at parks and boat ramps and ask me to take their picture next to the alligator warning sign. The signs used by the Florida Department of Environmental Protection say "CAUTION! / ALLIGATORS / NO SWIMMING." They feature a slash through a schematic swimmer and alligator head looking suitably subtle and greedy.

I like the use of the word "caution." It's a step down from the alarmist "danger" or harsh "warning." "Caution" suggests we need not get all jumpy. This is normal hereabouts. Just keep your head about you. In smaller letters it says: "WE ARE CONCERNED ABOUT WILDLIFE," and below that, "WE

ARE CONCERNED ABOUT PEOPLE." Nobody is taking sides here. The state of Florida is concerned about both. I appreciate that.

When a Florida tourist is deprived of the pleasure of spotting a live alligator, an alligator-warning sign is the next best thing. In a world of packaged tours, don't-leave-the-walkway nature trails, and formerly exotic places overrun with bus-tourists, signage like this can be the only thing in the visual record hinting that you've been somewhere interesting.

The last time somebody asked me to snap a photo beside a warning sign, it was a British tourist at St. Marks National Wildlife Refuge. (That sign had a simpler but still striking red message, saying only, "WARNING: ALLIGATORS" above a cartoon of a subtle, greedy alligator.) She asked me if this was normal.

"Is this normal?" is a question visitors often ask of Floridians. Many things here strike visitors as *not* normal, and I'm always flattered that people still think so. It reassures me that people still find us interesting. That we're not yet just like everywhere else. And whatever it is they question, if it's said with the right tone of incredulity, I will always assure them, yes, this is normal.

Like when a German tourist I met in Everglades National Park asked me, "Is this normal?" as we watched a congregation of alligators sunning themselves on the road. She meant was this an average roadside scene? I assured her it was. The whole place is lousy with alligators. She had spent a lot of money getting here, and I was here to assure her she had landed somewhere worth telling people about.

And here the Florida Legislature is working with me for a change. Like most Floridians, I was surprised in 1987 to discover that the alligator was not already our official state reptile, if not our official state living thing. We used to be known as the Alligator State until better marketing minds prevailed.

As is often the case in the state symbol business, it was a Florida elementary school classroom that came to our aid and petitioned the legislature to correct this omission. As with all such legislation, the road was not without its bumps. At one point Miami Beach Democratic Rep. Mike Friedman offered an amendment striking "alligator" from the state reptile designation and substituting "Jim Smith." Smith, Gov. Bob Martinez's chief of staff, had been a 1986 Democratic candidate for governor, saw how the winds were blowing, and switched parties. The amendment passed committee, but the alligator was quickly restored to its rightful place in the enactment. Smith was not made our official state reptile no matter what anyone says. There were so many worthier designees.

Martinez signed the bill declaring the new state symbol in a W. T. Moore Elementary School classroom on May 11, 1987, in Tallahassee, with the beaming teachers, fourth- and fifthgrade kids told to be on their best behavior, a small alligator, and television cameras looking on.

Some may question the enthusiasm with which the state has embraced a creature that kills and maims people. Even the federal government picked a national symbol that doesn't usually attack people. According to the Florida Fish and Wildlife Conservation Commission, the state averages about six unprovoked alligator attacks a year where people suffer serious alligator bites. This statistic doesn't count people who were injured because they messed with alligators on purpose. (It happens. Google "Florida man" along with "alligator.")

The number has risen slightly in recent years because more people are living around alligator habitat all the time. It's not like they're out looking for us.

Still, if alligators weren't dangerous, nobody would be impressed. Look at California—it put a bear on its flag. Cool choice. And if it were up to me, the state flag and that of the University of Florida Athletic Department would be pretty much indistinguishable.

Orange

Fruit

The Whole Orange Gets Its Due

The orange (*Citrus sinensis* and hybrids thereof) is hereby
designated the official fruit of Florida.

—Florida Statute 15.0315

I AM AN INDIFFERENT GARDENER. There is this part of my
backyard that I have allowed to revert to something like its
natural state. I live near a state park, so I have a rough idea
what the natural state looks like, and believe me, I'm getting
close.

Like the park rangers, I pull down invasive vines and cut
back ferns and palmettos—just light housekeeping. But I
make one exception to my philosophy of hands-off, survival-
of-the-fittest backyard management: the orange tree. The orange tree that I fertilized and tended. That I wrapped up lov-
ingly when I heard halfway-believable freeze warnings.

I tended my orange tree the way Shinto priests look after
small patches of rice near the temple: as a rite keeping me in
touch with my forebears and the mystic land-spirits. A living
link to a romanticized Florida past. A reenactment of a scene

that graced generations of postcards and state tourism ads. This is, after all, our official state fruit.

My orange tree survived hurricanes, freezes, mild neglect, blights and bugs, and kids hanging off it and yanking off fruit for more than a quarter century. Even as the other neighborhood trees fell one by one to freezes, winds, disease, and aggressive lawn-service workers, this one held on. Each winter it produced so much fruit that I'd give some away as holiday gifts. I'd hand it out by the bagful to family and friends. I laid it out for coworkers on break tables with a sign that said, "Free: genuine, nearly organic, home-grown local oranges."

On receiving a home-grown orange, Florida etiquette demands that you should act amazed and grateful, as though the supermarket variety is too inferior to acknowledge. Never, never compare them to the standardized orbs from California you find in the store. Comparing oranges to oranges is acceptable only in elementary-school math class. These are something special. Fruit with their own character. In this case, it was a legacy variety of orange. Delicious but unsuitable to commercial needs because they are thin-skinned and seedy. Much like the presenter himself.

But then, like about 80 percent of citrus in the state, my beloved tree fell victim to citrus greening. It didn't get ugly all at once, but after two successive years of sour, unevenly colored greenish fruit the size of ping-pong balls, something was horribly wrong. Still, the tart, diseased fruit was an excellent addition to old fashioneds. I had to admit it: these were terrible oranges. And so few.

"Cut it down," was the terse advice I got when I called a county agricultural agent for advice. He didn't need to hear the details. He'd been through this already from tree owners in various stages of denial. This disease had wiped out a shocking number of Florida citrus groves, yet somehow it was the backyard growers who were least able to accept the new, bleak citrus reality.

He told me that by leaving my beloved tree standing, I was personally contributing to the downfall of the state's orange industry. That's because when the bugs that spread this disease, the Asian citrus psyllids, happen by a sick tree, they feed on its leaves, soak up the disease bacteria, and carry these on to their next victim. I'd been sheltering a plague tree. I was part of the problem.

Once a tree is infected, "it's a goner," said the agent, with the weary tone of a cancer specialist laying out the hard facts to the family. Cut it back, and it will grow back diseased, he assured me. Assuming it would grow back at all, which was doubtful.

Harsh. How about planting tangerines? "Nope," he said. Same disease, same problem. Grapefruit? Same thing. It's called *citrus* greening, not orange greening. He suggested peaches. There are warmer weather varieties that like Florida just fine.

This was unacceptable. Peaches? This is Florida, damn it. And Florida has one and only one official state fruit: the fruit we display on our license plates. The fruit on our welcome-to-Florida roadway signage, the orange. Among our diverse pantheon of state symbols, this is the one that most completely evokes our history, our mythos. It's our spirit fruit.

Losing my pitiful backyard tree—now cut up and piled at the end of the driveway along with the debris from Hurricane Irma, a storm that blew away its last stunted and diseased fruit—meant the loss of one more personal connection with the Sunshine State Dream. I was not ready to be living in post-citrus Florida.

My own little town, Daytona Beach, first blossomed during that short, sunny nineteenth-century economic phenomenon that was called "orange fever." And a little to the west, incorporated during the height of orange fever, Orange City was founded and so named despite the skeptics. "They said we had neither oranges nor a city there," an early settler recalled. It was an aspirational name. Like Port Orange to my south, which didn't have a port as such but might if enough would-be orange growers were lured there by the name and some canny promotion. "The occupation of orange-growing has a tendency to make one hopeful for the future," proclaimed one Orange Fever Era agricultural guide. It's an attitude that outlasted the trees.

Central Florida flourished on that hopefulness. Remember that oranges carried more exotic associations in those pre-supermarket days. They were something you could only get seasonally. Just holding one in your gloved hand at a fruit stall on a sooty, icy, nineteenth-century northern city street seemed to whisper the promise of warmer, easier places a person could go. It was a dream that beckoned the newcomer with the kind of placid climate that offered smart operators a laidback path to easily reaped riches. Our fruit was always low-hanging.

Here is the promise as laid out in that same enthusiastic U.S. Department of Agriculture publication from 1882:

> To persons of foresight and capital, who are looking to the future rather than the present for remunerative

returns, Florida presents, in her orange pursuit, the most extended as well as the most inviting field. . . . It is not only a pleasing but an independent occupation. Its pursuit is no dead level of monotonous exertion, but one that affords scope for the development of an ingenious mind. As a producer, the orange grower is working under conditions of constantly increasing advantages.

None of this getting-up-before-dawn-to-milk-the-cows agriculture. You could grow rich while developing your ingenious mind, contemplating the natural scene from your fishing boat or hammock! Not exactly Jimmy Buffett lyrics, but one hears the same notes. And people responded. Especially people who had no idea what they were getting into. "It is amusing to see the recently settled lawyer, doctor or retired merchant or farmer attempt to take care of an orange grove, as he has been accustomed to develop an apple orchard in the North," a travel writer told readers in 1891.

The orange fever years—from the 1880s until the 1890s when freezes killed off the dream—brought an influx of people to the state and cemented the idea of Florida as a place where a man could make a killing without killing himself, or be healed from deadly illnesses, or just hang out and live easily off the land. Between the 1880 and 1900 censuses, the place almost doubled its population from 269,493 people to 528,542. We confidently strode into the twentieth century nearly the size of a real state.

Freezes, blights, and hurricanes cured the fever, but not our founding dream. Which makes it surprising that the Florida Legislature did not get around naming this as our official state fruit until 2005. It came about when fourth-graders at Southside Elementary in Sarasota noticed the omission and petitioned the legislature in 2004.

"Most people already think the orange is the official fruit, so we're putting into law what people already think is a law," explained the bill's Senate sponsor, Sen. Mike Haridopolos. If only more legislation were so self-evident.

The usual lame jokes were cracked about the state's surplus of official state symbols, which by then was thirty-four items and rising. Editorial writers huffed about the wasted time. And one senator attempted to use the bill as a vehicle for granting Key lime pie official state status. Nice try. But the orange blossom had been the state flower since 1909, and orange juice had been the state beverage since 1967: the legislature has been working toward this goal one piece of the orange tree at a time. It might as well finish the job and go full orange.

Gov. Jeb Bush signed the bill at Southside Elementary School on May 20, 2005. He talked about state symbols with the kids, handed out pens, and shook everyone's hand. "I've talked to everyone about this, and not a single person can believe we didn't have a state fruit, and that it wasn't the orange," he said. And noting that Florida was also the nation's lightning capital and potato chip capital, he suggested the work of official symbol-making was not finished. And certainly, children and future Floridians, it is not.

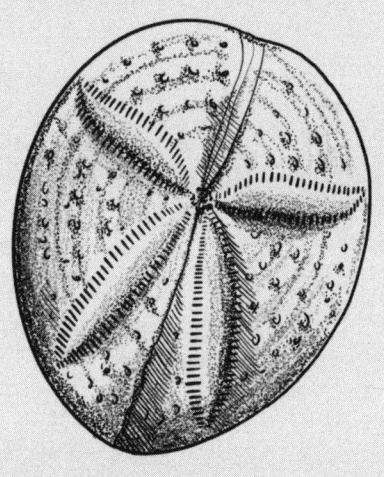

Eocene
Heart Urchin

Fossil

Pain in My Eocene Heart

The Eocene Heart Urchin, *Eupatagus antillarum*. This Late Eocene age irregular echinoid is similar to the heart urchins of modern tropical seas. It lived buried in the bottom sediments of the shallow seas that covered Florida 38 million years ago. The fossilized shell of this species is commonly found in the Ocala Limestone and Avon Park Formations. The Eocene Heart Urchin is designated the Florida state fossil.

—Senate Bill 676

AMONG STATE SEN. CHARLIE CLARY'S legislative accomplishments were getting a law named after his cute little dog (the Dixie Cup Clary Local Control Act) and getting within inches of bestowing Florida with an official state fossil. Into the 2006 bill that conferred official state pie status upon the beloved Key lime pie, the Destin Republican slipped an amendment honoring the Eocene heart urchin as the official state fossil and calcite as the official state mineral. But he withdrew the amendment, right before the final Senate vote.

This happened quickly and some missed the action. As a result, a few press reports at the time mentioned the appearance of a new official state fossil. You'll see the Eocene heart urchin referred to on websites and in books as the official state fossil. Yet sadly, we are a state bereft of an official state fossil.

Sure, we own a state stone, agatized coral, which is not actually a stone but a fossil. But I like the idea of an upfront for-real state fossil, and the Eocene heart urchin is as good as any. It's an irregular echinoid, which, this being Florida, is exactly the kind of echinoid that should represent us.

To an untrained eye, the Eocene heart urchin looks like any tourist shell-shop sea urchin except it's hard, smaller, and not round. It's the size and shape of a large, smooshed egg. They are found in limestone deposits as well as on eBay.

But having a state fossil is more politically tricky than you'd think. The Eocene epoch was between 56 and 34 million years ago. The planet was warmer then because the air had lots more carbon dioxide. And Florida was underwater. Hmmm, you may say, what if some future age also had lots more carbon dioxide in the air and made the planet warmer—wouldn't a lot of the state be underwater again? Controversial musings in a time when sea-level rise is an uncomfortable topic in Tallahassee. Gov. Rick Scott had put the phrase "global warming" on the Florida Department of Environmental Protection's Index of Forbidden Phrases.

In those globally warm, long-ago watery times, there was a shallow seabed where the north-central part of the state is now. That's where those little Eocene heart urchins frolicked. A lot of them, judging from all the fossilized remains that show up in limestone pits. As the seas receded, the limestone shallows became islands—Orange Island, geologists call that first big, emerging Florida land mass—and Florida rose from the ocean.

But if you want to celebrate the humble little Eocene heart urchin, you could find yourself sliding not only into troubling issues like global sea levels but the idea that the earth must be a very old place if these urchins managed to get themselves fossilized. And that slides effortlessly into other troubling matters like mass extinctions, evolution, and worse. If you doubt that these matters are still controversial, remember that in 2012, when asked about the age of the planet in an interview, Florida Sen. Marco Rubio's flight response was triggered. "I'm not a scientist, man," he replied. Oh, bless your Eocene heart, Rubio.

A cool fossil and a nice little paperweight, but such baggage! This is why I wouldn't expect to see any legislator going to bat for the Eocene heart anytime soon. A shame. Florida needs an official state fossil.

OFFICIAL MARINE MAMMAL

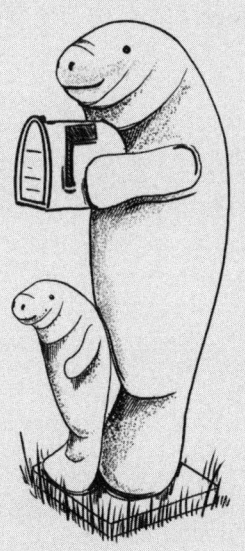

Manatee

Marine Mammal

Welcome to the Land of the Manatee Mailboxes

The manatee, also commonly known as the sea cow,
is hereby designated the Florida state marine mammal.

—Florida Statute 15.038

A BENEFIT OF THE TIME I SPEND on a bicycle is a sharpened awareness of the neighborhood. I smell things I wouldn't smell inside a car and can sense a barbecue a half mile away. I'm more aware of garage sales and the dog and cat populations. And I notice mailboxes more. A lot more.

Because they're just below a cyclist's eye level, mailboxes are landmarks on any regular route. Turn left after the dolphin mailbox. Hang a right after the open-mouth bass mailbox. You're halfway home at the manatee mailbox.

I take particular pleasure in manatee mailboxes. They are cultural markers, too. A place that has a lot of them is a part of the state where I'm likely to feel at home. This has never steered me wrong. A place where they are banned, discouraged, ridiculed, or out of character, conversely, is a place where I'd likely not feel welcome and won't linger.

Florida does not have an official state mailbox (I know, why not?), but if a lot of people have erected mailbox tributes to a creature, that creature must have some claim on us. And the two creatures most regularly and widely honored as mail receptacles are manatees and dolphins. Yes, the occasional bass, too, but they're way smaller and represent less of a commitment on the part of the homeowner. Sadly, we have no hard data from the Census Bureau or the Postal Service on mailbox themes.

Actually the phrase "manatee mailbox" is a misnomer. It's the mailbox holder that's in the shape and likeness of a West Indian manatee. Usually the beast is smiling and clutching a conventional mailbox between its flippers as though presenting a gift.

The holders range from fancier weather-resistant, mail-order fiberglass sculptures to crude, homemade concrete or plaster approximations. These don't tax a sculptor's skill. They're basically the Pillsbury Doughboy or Stay Puft Marshmallow Man with a head pinched into a snout and arms and legs pinched into flippers.

The top mailbox animals were all added to the official state menagerie in 1975. State Sen. Bob Graham, who would later become governor and U.S. senator while remaining a friend of the manatee, filed a bill to name the manatee as the state marine mammal and "the porpoise, also commonly known as the dolphin, is hereby designated as the Florida state saltwater mammal." Anyone who watched the television show *Flipper* on a regular basis knows porpoises and dolphins are different creatures and that the beloved icon holding mailboxes along coastal Florida is a smiling bottlenose dolphin, and not a porpoise. But never you mind, when the Florida Legislature's heart is in the right place, one does not gainsay.

Other bills in that notable session named the Florida large-mouth bass as the official state freshwater fish and the Atlantic sailfish as the official state saltwater fish. Worthy choices. Many Floridians express their fondness for the bass with their mailboxes. And many waterfront grills proudly display sailfish, both in fiberglass and taxidermized forms, over their bars. Customers expect it.

But whereas a bass mailbox proclaims a certain expertise and avocation on the part of the homeowner, and a dolphin (not a porpoise) mailbox suggests a sports alliance, a manatee mailbox commits you to nothing. You're hanging loose and identifying with animals that float around noiselessly in the water not bothering anybody except boaters who should be powering down anyway and appreciating where they are. An excellent fit with the Florida coastal dweller's ethos.

Among Florida's 122 specialty license plates—always significant cultural markers—the "Save the Manatee" plate ranked number 6 at the end of 2018, just below the dolphin (not porpoise) plates. There were 47,117 cars displaying manatee license plates that year, or roughly six of them for every living manatee.

The plate is popular in western Volusia County because this is home to Blue Spring, a place where hundreds of manatees flock whenever the water gets cold. The water in the spring is reliably around 72 degrees—too cold for Floridians but a lifesaver for manatees, which get stressed when river temperatures drop below 68 degrees.

In the natural order of things, it is not winter in Volusia County until manatees return to Blue Spring in numbers.

And with the return of the manatees comes the return of even larger numbers of manatee watchers. Starting around Christmastime, the park's parking lot can reach capacity before lunchtime with a line of cars forming at the gate. Nearby Orange City has a manatee festival in February. Christmas and manatee festival time are the only days when Orange City dwellers wish for cold weather.

Blue Spring is a place where the edge of natural Florida borders the sprawl radiating from Orlando. The park used to be at the end of a dirt road in the middle of nowhere but now shows evidence of being loved to death. When I was a kid there used to be a rope tied to an oak limb overlooking the boil so you could swing and drop, Tarzan-style, into the clear water below. Now there's a viewing platform on that spot with a tartly worded sign warning about soil erosion.

Still, it's hard to argue with the place's appeal during manatee-watching season. And manatee watching at Blue Spring has many things to recommend it over bird watching. First, it does not require study. Florida has some five hundred bird species but only one manatee species, the West Indian manatee. If a tourist asks what kind of manatee is that over there, you can confidently say, "That one looks to me like a West Indian manatee," and your questioner will nod appreciatively.

Also, manatee watching does not require quick reflexes. "Holy shit! A red-speckled, blue-billed, pileated Goode tern! (The immature plumage throws people off)," someone will shout, and you'll spin around and see an empty oak branch. Manatee watching doesn't require any more quickness of eye than rock collecting. They sit there. You sit there. I find this an ideal arrangement.

Finally, manatee watching does not require binoculars. Nature encourages birds to be small. But if your eyesight is good enough to spot a Coke machine at twenty paces, you are equipped to spot manatees.

To locate manatees at Blue Spring, look for a clump of four or more tourists who appear unrelated and are staring into the water. That was how I found my first sighting of the season.

"Is it dead?" the man on the dock asked nobody in particular.

Always a plausible enough assumption. The creature was inert in shallow water. As with nearly all manatees, its back looked like an urban road map. In this case it had a major highway of a beige scar about the width of a bicycle tire. Boaters killed 119 manatees in 2017.

"He looks awful!" ventured the woman wrapped in a Mickey Mouse towel who tried calling to it: "Whooze, whooze, whooze!"

As if to settle the question, the creature stuck its doglike snout a half-inch above the water's surface, flared its nostrils, exhaled, inhaled, and returned to repose on the river bottom. The watchers were visibly relieved and called the kids over.

Guessing whether their subjects are alive is a hot topic of conversation among the manatee watchers. Helpful hint: To give the illusion of being a manatee expert, reassure the other watchers the creature in question is alive, even nimble by the blimplike standards of the species. It should take a good half hour for anyone to discover if you were wrong, and by then everyone will have left.

I moved on to the gift store and walked past manatee coffee mugs, manatee beer-bottle openers, manatee T-shirts, manatee spoons, manatee koozies, manatee bumper stickers, and stuffed manatees to buy a manatee refrigerator magnet and some Christmas-tree ornaments showing a contented manatee wearing a Santa Claus hat. These ornaments are not widely available outside the state. I like to send them as holiday gifts to friends up north, hoping they will find them baffling and exotic—exactly the image I try to promote for my home. Seasons greetings from the Land of the Manatee Mailboxes.

OFFICIAL STATE SOIL

Myakka

Soil

Myakka Fine Sand, and a Fine Sand It Is

Myakka fine sand (sandy, siliceous, hyperthermic *Aeric Haplaquods*) is hereby designated and declared as the official Florida state soil.

—Florida Statute 15.047

I was giving a talk at a garden show and somebody from the county extension office came over to me with a big jar of sand. Dirty sand, coarse and gray with what looked like pepper sprinkled through it.

"You know what this is?" he asked.

I didn't. But as a self-appointed Florida studies expert, I can sense when somebody is testing my bona fides.

I brazened it out. "That's our official state soil!" I exclaimed.

"Well, right you are," he said, evidently glad to be talking to somebody who knew the dirt around here. "Myakka fine sand!"

"And a fine sand it is," I agreed.

Myakka fine sand is the state's most common soil. It's a sand, but not a beach sand. It's the kind of sand you might tap off your shoes walking through slash pine forests and palmetto scrubs. An inland sand found almost everywhere except southern Florida and covering some 1.5 million acres.

The Myakka fine sand bill became a cause for soil scientist Frank Watts. Watts had heard that Wisconsin had picked an official state soil (Antigo silt loam) in 1983, and he felt Florida should do likewise to raise a little appreciation for soil science and the wonders beneath our feet. For his labors, he would get referred to in print as "Mr. Myakka."

In 1988 Watts found a sponsor in the Senate, and he delivered a speech at a subcommittee hearing, a speech in which he laid out the unheralded work of soil scientists, lauded the geological richness we stand on in Florida, and asked people not to dismiss it all as mere dirt. A cri de coeur from the natural sciences.

Was this appreciated? No, it was not. There ensued a lot of cheap ridicule about dirt. The bill stalled in Senate committee. Another Senate sponsor had to be found the next year because the sponsor, Sen. Wayne Hollingsworth, wasn't re-elected. His opponent slammed him for not having enough clout even to get the state soil bill out of his own committee.

Naturally, other candidates for state soil also were put forward at this point, because hey, you're leaving out South Florida and coastal areas here. How about Everglades muck? How about Astatula sand? And as they do whenever a new state symbol law is debated, editorial pages and newspaper columnists giggled and suggested tongue-in-cheek substitutes (Everglades muck, heck, why not fill dirt?) and asked the unanswerable political question, "Why are we even doing this?"

But the full force of the Florida Association of Professional Soil Classifiers remained behind the bill. In terms of clout, they're not exactly the National Rifle Association, but these are the people who know this stuff. And they sold T-shirts saying, "Support Myakka fine sand/Florida state soil." Whenever T-shirts appear, you know an issue has arrived. This was practically a movement.

Supporting it, too, was Agriculture Commissioner Doyle Connor, who was probably the most widely known Florida officeholder other than governor because his name was on every gas pump for three decades, assuring you the counter on the device would indeed start at zero. Even Sen. Hollingsworth's successor came around.

The bill passed in 1989 and Governor Bob Martinez signed it into law on May 22. "Saving the soil is no joke," the *Florida Times-Union* solemnly editorialized on the occasion as it blessed the newest addition to the state's pantheon of symbols.

This is the state soil you're laughing about, wiseacres! Yeah, you in the back! But yes, people still chuckle when you tell them we have statutorily recognized state soil. Me, I love the idea. It has no cultural or historical baggage; it advances nobody's commercial interest; and it asks us to take a second to regard average, not terribly productive soil as something upon which everything rests.

OFFICIAL STATE DAY

April 2nd

Florida Day

Ponce de Leon Schlepped Here!

(1) April 2 of each year is hereby designated as "Florida State Day." The day to be known as "Pascua Florida Day."

(2) The Governor may annually issue a proclamation designating April 2 as said State Day and designating the week of March 27 to April 2 as "Pascua Florida Week" and calling upon public schools and citizens of Florida to observe the same as a patriotic occasion.

—Florida Statute 683.06

I GOT THE PRESS RELEASE for the unveiling of the statue of Juan Ponce de Leon at the parking lot of the Guana Tolomato Matanzas Estuarine Research Reserve, an event that was to take place on Florida State Day, but I only made it out there afterward. The statue was erected to commemorate the 500th anniversary of Ponce de Leon's first landfall in Florida on April 2, 1513, the day when, in a less enlightened age, Florida was said to have been "discovered." Someplace within roughly three hundred miles or so of this very spot, Spanish explorers trod the sand, gave thanks to their God, and looked around for aboriginals so they could ask what a guy had to do to find a little gold around here.

The bronze Spaniard is shown pointing westward, in the direction of the nature trail, which is also open to mountain bikes, nicely shaded, and has places to sit and watch birds. I recommend it. I suspect, though, his pose says something more metaphorical than "this way to the trailhead."

The six-foot statue is atop a pedestal tall enough for tourists to spot from State Road A1A. There's a similar bronze in Punta Gorda, near the place where the explorer was fatally wounded by a poisoned arrow on his second Florida expedition. The West Coast natives understood early in the game that being discovered was not going to work for them.

Another Ponce de Leon statue stands at the end of the Bridge of Lions in St. Augustine in honor of St. Augustine's claim of being the spot where Ponce de Leon first waded ashore to Florida. And because the Ancient City can't emphasize this point enough, there are even more Ponce de Leon statues at the Fountain of Youth Archaeological Park out by U.S. Highway 1.

In honor of the 500th anniversary, still another statue went up near Melbourne Beach, also marking the spot where Ponce de Leon first came ashore. He's depicted facing the ocean and holding a cross aloft as though warding off vampires.

And between the northern statues in St. Augustine and the southern statue in Melbourne Beach is the statueless Ponce de Leon Inlet, renamed by legislative memorial in 1927 because—you guessed it—it's the spot where Ponce de Leon came ashore in Florida. The claim may not be true, but what was incontestable was that the old name, Mosquito Inlet, dating from the sixteenth century, represented remarkably bad marketing. The Great Florida Land Boom had fizzled out by that time and banks were failing. Floridians met these challenges the way we always have in times of adversity: we pick ourselves up, dust ourselves off, and say out loud, "Time to rebrand." Or words to that effect.

Maritime historian Samuel Eliot Morison lent cred to all this by declaring that Ponce de Leon Inlet looked about right to him, but local historians already had been running with the inlet's claim to first contact for some time. Florian Mann, founder of the *Halifax Journal,* wrote, published, and sold by subscription and mail order ($1.50, postpaid) a fictionalized Ponce de Leon bio that had the explorer landing in St. Augustine but quickly heading to New Smyrna Beach and then tromping another twenty miles to West Volusia seeking the Fountain of Youth.

This purported westward trek also gave us a town and a state park named DeLeon Springs. In the 1950s and '60s tourists arriving at DeLeon Springs Park were greeted with a larger-than-life-sized painted plaster statue of Ponce de Leon, clad in armor and arm-in-arm with a blonde in a one-piece bathing suit. Our glorious past united with our babealicious present. It was an impressive artwork.

Melbourne Beach insists it has the strongest case for being Ponce de Leon's landing site. In 1990 Douglas Peck, retired Air Force pilot, amateur historian, writer, sailor, bon vivant, and all-around colorful Florida guy, retraced Ponce de Leon's first Florida voyage in a thirty-three-foot cutter. He corrected for known compass errors, compared what he encountered to the accounts from the time, and declared that our discoverer arrived at a site "28 degrees north latitude and 80 degrees, 29 minutes, west longitude, which is south of Cape Canaveral and a short distance south of Melbourne Beach. I do not say that this is the exact spot, but I place the accuracy within five to eight nautical miles either side of this fix." Close enough for another statue.

Despite all the statuary, Florida State Day is not much celebrated beyond the city limits of St. Augustine. And no wonder. Where other places have founding stories that celebrate brave pioneers and determined settler-forebears, Floridians are left with the guys who helped wipe out the local indigenous cultures that had been here some 12,000 years without bothering anybody, and who having done that, packed up and gave up on the place.

Still, Ponce de Leon did leave us with a nice name—"the state with the prettiest name," as poet Elizabeth Bishop rightly observed. We could have been named after some random saint or some bit of wildlife he and his crew noticed: Mosquitoland, Land of Serpents, or something. We might have been noted on maps as the Land of Swamps Without a Damn Speck of Gold. Instead, because it was Eastertime, we were named for Pascua Florida, Feast of the Flowers. Nice touch. Born at the right time.

birthday of Robert E. Lee : 1-19
Confederate Memorial Day : 4-26
birthday of Jefferson Davis : 6-3

Holidays

Lost Holidays of the Lost Cause Linger

(1) The legal holidays, which are also public holidays, are the following: . . . (d) Birthday of Robert E. Lee, January 19. . . . (j) Confederate Memorial Day, April 26. . . . (l) Birthday of Jefferson Davis, June 3.

—Florida Statute 683.01

FLORIDA RECOGNIZES A SLEW OF HOLIDAYS. Florida Statute 683.01 lists twenty, which are supplemented by twenty-seven other special days of varying import. Most are fake holidays that wouldn't even give a bank teller a day at the beach.

From Arbor Day to I Am an American Day, from Pascua Florida Day to Gasparilla Day, this is an ignored page in the Florida statute book. But during the 2018 legislative session, holidays became the subject of caffeinated public comment. On February 6, 2018, the Senate Community Affairs Committee voted 4–2 to approve a bill that would remove three seldom-observed holidays from the books: Robert E. Lee's birthday, January 19; Confederate Memorial Day, April 26; and Jefferson Davis's birthday, June 3.

None of these grants a day off anymore. A long time ago, maybe. Especially in North Florida. Where I live, banks in Daytona Beach observed Confederate Memorial Day, Jefferson Davis's birthday, and Robert E. Lee's birthday as late as the 1950s, but the practice soon died out. Even so, as far back as 1915, the *Daytona Daily News* noted that like most of Central and South Florida, "In Daytona, where the population is overwhelmingly made up of people from northern states, no formal observance of Confederate Memorial Day is made."

The legislature made Confederate Memorial Day a legal holiday back in 1895. It's celebrated on April 26, which is the anniversary of Gen. Joseph E. Johnston's surrender to Gen. William T. Sherman. As Karen Cox documented in her book *Dixie's Daughters,* getting this holiday on calendars across the South had been a major project of the United Daughters of the Confederacy since the end of the nineteenth century. And at the end of the nineteenth and beginning of the twentieth centuries, these were ladies to whom North Florida legislators listened respectfully and replied "yes'm" when they were quite done. Davis's holiday took longer to get on the books. It wasn't enacted until 1905.

Traditionally Florida has cultivated a mixed and selective attitude toward its closet full of Confederate symbols. Unlike neighboring states, the Florida Way strives for a kind of Southern Lite—some of the flavor, less of the hangover. The Confederate flag that used to be outside the Florida Capitol flew alongside other flags from the state's past, giving the display a measure of deniability. And when Gov. Jeb Bush quietly shunted the whole thing off to the Florida Museum of History in 2001, nobody noticed for days; an indication of how lightly Floridians regarded the issue.

But lately neo-Nazis, Ku Klux Klan members, and white nationalists in bad haircuts have been rallying to the symbols and statuary of the old breakaway Southern republic. And this has forced communities across the South to take a hard, new look at these symbols and what they stand for. Sen. Lauren Book, a Democrat from the unfortunately named town of Plantation, filed a bill to remove the holidays from the statute books. "Our history is rich and undeniable, and no one is seeking to erase that," she said. "However, I believe we must underscore diversity and undercut tributes that celebrate the Confederacy, which upheld the institution of slavery and perpetuated inequality and division in our country."

Among committee members voting against the bill was Thonotosassa Republican Sen. Tom Lee, who cited "a flood of phone calls from people that were offended by us." He didn't see any harm in the holidays, especially since few people bothered to note them, and the few who did seemed to feel strongly about the matter. "I didn't think the juice was worth the squeeze," he told reporters. And, well, Lee was also contemplating a run for statewide office that year, and there was undoubtedly a bloc of Republican primary voters out there who shed tears on Confederate Memorial Day.

The vote came after an emotional hearing. Best pull-quote from speakers: "This is cultural genocide." Another said Gen. Lee is spoken of as Godlike. Not even the neo-Confederate fan base speaks of Davis as divine, but they expressed support for his day too, because he was part of the package. Being president of a breakaway republic was a thankless job but somebody had to do it.

In the last week of the session the Senate Governmental Oversight and Accountability Committee chair also decided the juice was not worth the squeeze, killing the measure. Which means the state statute book continues to be littered with monuments to the War of the Rebellion. Did you know Florida also has Confederate flag anti-desecration statutes? Yup, one that forbids commercial use. No exception for T-shirts or bikinis, either. Fortunately for the southern T-shirt industry, that statute lacks penalties.

The Florida Legislature had once again wrestled with the ghosts of the Confederacy and the ghosts won. In the world of Florida symbolic politics, they often do.

OFFICIAL STATEHOOD DAY

March 3, 1845

State Day

Florida Statehood Day Oration

Be it enacted by the Senate and House of Representatives of the United States of America in Congress assembled, that the States of Iowa and Florida be, and the same are hereby, declared to be States of the United States of America, and are hereby admitted into the Union on equal footing with the original States, in all respects whatsoever. . . . APPROVED, March 3, 1845.

—An Act for the Admission of the States of Iowa
and Florida into the Union.

HELLO? IS THIS EVERYBODY? Well, too bad, they'll find their way in here. The newspaper ran the right time for a change, and we might as well start because the yoga class has reserved the room for exactly a half hour from now. Let me warn you, for people teaching inner calm they can be a pushy bunch.

Welcome and happy Florida Statehood Day, March 3. I'm not surprised at the lack of turnout here. You in the back, come up here so I don't have to shout. This microphone barely works. As I said, I'm not surprised at the turnout because hardly anybody knows this is Florida's Statehood Day.

Nobody gets this day off, which is galling because early March is too nice a time for people to be cooped up in offices and classrooms. It nicely coincides with Daytona Beach's Bike Week, too.

But hey, Florida is a place that lives in the happy, perennially sunny present and isn't much interested in anything that happened before the last Spring Break. Plus talking about statehood means getting into not only ancient lore from the Time Before Disney but also uncomfortable ancient lore from the Time Before Disney.

We forget that not everybody in Florida—probably not even the majority—was into the whole statehood project when the territory petitioned Congress to join the club in 1844. This meant that joining the Union took a little of the good ol' electoral engineering for which our state is famous. People on the eastern shoreline were not into becoming a state and especially not into being a state with those people in West Florida.

Applying the traditional What's in It for Us Test, East Coasters concluded that statehood meant a lot of expense and responsibility without much by way of benefits. And they had a point. Florida didn't have enough people or a big enough economy to be a for-real state. This meant things could get expensive fast.

And then there was that whole peninsular-Florida-versus-panhandle-Florida tension, a constant in Florida politics up to our own day. The English had wisely set apart East Florida and West Florida as the two different places they are. Which suited East Florida people just fine.

"The God of Nature made the Suwannee River the division line or boundary between East and West Florida," declared one East Florida petition to the Congress, as though this were an obvious thing that needed to be pointed out for the benefit of dim out-of-towners. It's the natural order. God knows and everybody else knows what the deal is down here.

Worse, if you start having a state, then you start having a state legislature. A legislature that would start making laws because that's what legislatures do. And before you'd know it, you'd have all these West and Middle Florida types making rules, levying taxes, hiring relatives, and worst of all, chartering banks.

You think people hate banks now? That's nothing compared to the Andrew Jackson–era South. Good Floridian country folk thought compound interest and the bond market were scams and devil magic. And not without reason. Banks in those days had the habit of folding their tents and slipping out of town like the circus.

But the pro-statehood people got out in front of that parade and campaigned as being even more anti-bank than their opponents. And to show they meant business, the pro-statehood delegates who wrote the state's 1838 constitution barred bank employees from holding state elected office. Bankers, duelists, and "persons convicted of bribery, perjury, or other infamous crimes," were declared to be people you can't trust with public office. The voters bought it.

The slavery divide also complicated things. East Florida supported slavery. West Florida really, really supported slavery. And mid-Florida really, really, really supported slavery. Naturally, this difference of opinion sparked hot disagreement.

But slavery was the whole reason East and West Florida would be joined together in holy statehood. Iowa was going to apply for admission to the Union, and that meant southerners in Congress had to rustle up another slave state in a hurry to keep things balanced. There were barely enough people in Florida for one state, let alone two. So if statehood was going to happen, the two Floridas had to become one. No matter how much bellyaching was heard in St. Augustine.

Iowa and Florida then got rolled into one statehood bill. Nobody could vote for the free state without getting a slave state in the bargain. Pretty slick.

But if Florida was going to be a state, it needed a state constitution, and the constitutional referendum that ensued was a familiar Florida story—disputed voting rules, a razor-thin victory margin, and results not everybody accepted as real. If you read any account of the vote, you'll notice the authors often fudge the vote total. That's because nobody knows what it was.

The territorial government announced several victory margins for the final vote on the state constitution in 1839, the last electoral step to statehood. Maybe it passed by 113 votes, maybe 95 votes, or maybe 20-something votes, or maybe it didn't actually pass at all—depends on who you talk to. And even this narrow victory came about after tabulators threw out ballots that said things like "no state" and "no convention" because technically it was only a state constitution they were voting on, and not statehood itself. Voter intent didn't matter overmuch in this operation.

The territorial governor, Robert Reid, a big supporter of statehood, didn't get around to giving the final figures until a year and nine months after the election and sounded testy about the flack he was getting over the lack of any official count. He objected that he had only been required to announce which side won and not a bunch of *details* about it. Sheesh.

From what was finally divulged about the 1841 tally of the 1839 vote, it seems even western Florida was divided on a constitution and statehood, although it had previously been all for the idea. Eastern Florida was against statehood and being hooked up with West Florida. And the areas in between—where the capital would be and where people were in the slaphappy throes of a land boom (a boom that, in true Florida fashion, residents imagined would go on more or less forever)—tipped the balance in favor.

Because of these ancient fights and ballot-counting prestidigitations, we're stuck with a state capital deep in the middle of nowhere that nobody can get to without driving most of the day and encountering a lot of zero-tolerance speed-limit enforcement. A state capital that would house a legislature that supported secession, our gimcrack 1885 state constitution, Jim Crow, the use of prisoners as rent-a-slaves, prohibition, public education on the cheap, extravagant public land giveaways to railroads, boisterous over-development, the draining of the Everglades, and whatever morals legislation was being talked up on the revival circuit in any given year. I stew over this every time I drive four hours to Tallahassee.

So thanks, state founding fathers. Thanks a bunch. Thanks for the drive and Baker County's speed-limit enforcement on Interstate 10. Thanks for yoking together Panama City Beach and Miami Beach. No wonder we, as a state, ignore this holiday and try to talk about something more pleasant each time March 3 rolls around.

Thanks for listening, folks. Have a happy Florida Statehood Day; celebrate it by having a beer someplace in sight of the water. I'd order oysters, too, because March has an "R" in it, and this means oysters are allowed, something Statehood Day has over the Fourth of July. And go fold your chairs and put them against the wall on your way out. I can't do everything around here.

Official State Play

Cross and Sword

Play

Men in Tights with Cross and Sword

The historical pageant by Paul Green known as the "Cross and Sword," presented annually by the citizens of the City of St. Augustine, is hereby designated the official play of the state.

—Florida Statue 15.036

FAKE BEARDS! Rippling banners! Flashing lights! Campfire dancing! Cannon fire! Conquistadors! A tree-shaking hurricane! Flagler College students cavorting in flesh-colored leotards and Spanish moss! Men in tights declaiming! An Indian princess! What's not to love about *Cross and Sword?* "A symphonic outdoor drama based on early Florida history," as it was styled right there on its program.

The play hasn't been performed since 1996. Sadly, symphonic outdoor dramas based on early history aren't the draw they used to be. The amphitheater where it was headquartered is now a concert venue. ZZ Top played there, so did Bob Dylan, even Little Richard.

Still, the state play is missed. Not so much by theatergoers but by St. Augustine residents, especially students. Its program in its final year listed 47 actors and dancers, 33 staffers and stagehands, and 23 interns. And even that impressive troupe was less than half the size of the cast the play employed in its early years. Extras in armor and robes were hired to go out into the tourist attractions of St. Augustine to drum up a little business, too. It was a fantastic summer job. A theater-camp kid can't find work like that anymore.

As anyone who saw the movie *Waiting for Guffman* knows, this nation has a rich tradition of pageant-style theater about local history and founding stories. And as the city in America with the oldest founding story, St. Augustine felt ripe for its own symphonic outdoor drama based on its early history.

Cross and Sword was conceived by the man who invented the symphonic outdoor drama genre, Paul Green. His first such play, *The Lost Colony*, opened with the help of the New Deal's Works Progress Administration in 1937 and is still performed in North Carolina. It was a hit with tourists and was soon imitated by other aspiring tourist towns.

Unfortunately, St. Augustine's founding story is not an uplifting story of hardy pioneers triumphing over adversity and hewing a city out of the wilderness. It's about a state-sponsored military expedition that brought European religious wars to the New World, followed by the eradication of the indigenous people encountered. This is not whistling-the-songs-on-the-way-out history. It's sad history, not uplifting WPA-mural history.

The steely Don Pedro Menendez de Aviles who was on a mission from God is not a man who humanizes easily. Not even with a cross-cultural romance with an Indian princess. Besides, he scooted out of town by the end of the show. Other places enjoyed pageants with valiant pioneers, Civil War reenactments, and based-on-a-local-folk-story symphonic outdoor dramas. But neither tourists nor locals outside St. Augustine identify much with Florida's story as the place where the Spanish Conquest foundered.

The problems celebrating Florida's colonial Spanish heritage can pop up in unexpected places in Florida. In the county immediately south of *Cross and Sword* land, the Flagler County School District built Matanzas High School in 2005, and some parents objected to the name. It seemed an obvious enough name. The school was near Matanzas Inlet, the Matanzas River, and Matanzas Woods golf course. But the word in Spanish means "slaughters" or "massacres," which meant the school's name sounded like a Spanglish title for a teen slasher movie: *Matanzas High School II: Home Room Horror!*

These objections were heard and waved off, and nobody much thought of them again, but the controversy did provide a teachable moment about local history. One that was news to most of the parents and kids. Palm Coast, home to Matanzas High School, was incorporated in 1999, so anything that happened there before the Clinton administration is considered half-disbelieved ancient history spoken of by the Old Ones. The pathfinding pioneer families arrived in the 1970s.

The place-name Matanzas comes from the inlet north of the high school, where in 1565 troops under Menendez executed nearly 250 French Protestant prisoners. Systematically, ten at a time, their hands bound behind them. It's the sort of thing that gives faith-based initiatives a bad name.

After the killings the Spanish government did hear from a few complainers who suggested this was going too far. But the crown brushed off the liberals and praised Menendez for a muscular, proactive, zero-tolerance policy toward Protestantism and French intruders. Now he's celebrated as the founder of St. Augustine. There's a Menendez Birthday Festival held there each February. But don't worry, nobody gets hurt. And he has a high school named after him, too. Pedro Menendez High School. Go Falcons!

Yet as raw material for an uplifting symphonic outdoor drama based on early history, the problems are obvious. And they were compounded by the timing of St. Augustine's 400th birthday.

The year 1964, St. Augustine's 399th birthday, was marked by racial protests, Ku Klux Klan violence, swim-ins, mass arrests, and the jailing of Martin Luther King Jr. for attempting to eat at the segregated Monson Motor Lodge Restaurant. After the court rulings came down, the arrests were processed, and the out-of-town press and King left town, St. Augustine's business community, the governor, and state tourist industry leaders were very much hoping to change the conversation and launch the state's 400th anniversary with a splash. A big play in a big new amphitheater with a huge cast and heroic themes set in a time that antedated, and therefore sidestepped, the whole institutionalized racial slavery thing in the South, filled the bill nicely.

The play was an immediate draw. Some 36,000 people saw it in 1965, its first year. Attendance grew in the 1970s. Richard Boone, star of the *Have Gun–Will Travel* television Western, who had moved to St. Augustine, appeared in newspaper ads around the state, was membership chair, helped with the production, and generally raised the play's profile. It became a popular school field trip. And in 1972 the legislature designated *Cross and Sword* the official state play.

But by the 1980s the production was in decline. In its last scaled-back year it drew an audience of fewer than 10,000 for the whole season. And really, the script didn't age well. Consider its Prince Valiant-y language ("Long, long ago, the dreamers walked this land. The strong of arm, the fond of heart, the valiant, and the daring . . ."). Then there were the strained uplift, Hollywood-style Native Americans, Big Indian Dance Numbers, and corny plot conventions with strained coincidences, and leaden comic relief didn't cut it even for an audience recruited from the Ancient City Tourist Trolley. Sad but true.

But it's still our official state play by statute. Something I see as less about the play itself than about a kind of celebration of pre-Disney tourism. Just off State Road A1A and south of the alligator farm. More impressive and educational than your usual tropical garden and orange juice stand. A strategy for climbing out of the swamp of bitter-ender segregationist local politics, a way to plant our banners on a better beach. Not by looking to the future but by embracing our not-very-embraceable founding story for the amusement of tourists and employment of locals. Yea verily and exit through the gift shop!

Swanee River

The Swanee River

Song

Florida's Official Ol' Plantation Song

Be it resolved by the House of Representatives of the State of Florida, the Senate concurring: That, from and after the adoption of this amendment the official song of the State of Florida, to be sung in the schools and at all other public or official gatherings, shall be "The Swanee River (Old Folks at Home)," written by Stephen Foster and entered according to an Act of Congress by Firth Pond & Co. in 1851, in the Clerk's office of the District Court of the Southern District of New York.

—House Concurrent Resolution 22 (1935)

WHEN CHARLIE CRIST WAS INAUGURATED as Florida governor in 2007, he broke with tradition by dispensing with a singing of the official state song. Instead he went with "The Florida Song" by Charles Atkins of the Florida State University's Blues Lab. The piece has a cool, gospel feel and is a great improvement over other attempts at a state song, which is to say it's not terrible.

Florida's state song, "Old Folks at Home," also called "Swanee River" or "Way Down Upon the Swanee River," had been a problem song for a long time. It was written by a composer who never visited Florida and misspelled the river's name. Stephen Foster found the name in an atlas and felt it sounded better than his first choice, the Pee Dee River, which it certainly does.

The lyrics are a lament for better times long gone, a weird choice for a state where the economy and ethos are based on the belief that we live in a paradise with real estate values poised to rocket. A line like "All the world am sad and dreary, eb-rywhere I roam" straddles the line between wistful melancholy and clinical depression. *All* the world? Even Disney World?

Then there's the next line: "Oh, darkies, how my heart grows weary . . ." Hoo boy, that's where you've entered the gates of Civil War Land and the reason Crist dispensed with it. Once you take this song out of storage and dust it off—well, you've paddled off the spring-fed Suwannee River and into the dark swamp of southern racial history.

"Frankly, I didn't want to be inaugurated to a minstrel song whose lyrics included 'darkies' and 'still longing for the old plantation,' . . . that wasn't exactly the inclusive message I had in mind," Crist later recalled.

"Old Folks at Home" is an 1851 minstrel tune, or "Ethiopian melody," as the song's first appearance in sheet music form styled it, which means it's saddled with all the burnt-cork, fake dialect, antebellum baggage of the genre. The song was reworded for Gov. Reubin Askew's inauguration and again for Gov. Jeb Bush's, so that the proceedings might sound a little less like a Confederate camp reenactment. For Bush's audience, the narrator was longing for "the old connection" instead of "de old plantation." It only kind of worked. As John Oliver joked on *Last Week Tonight*, "somehow it sounds racist today even in instrumental form."

The song sounds racist, lacks the strut necessary for a marching band arrangement, is sad, emphasizes the state's role as home to old folks, and has roughly zero to do with anything about post–Civil War Florida south of Interstate Highway 10. Other than that, it's a perfect song to represent the state. How did this happen?

Florida's previous state song was "Florida, My Florida," chosen in 1913. It's sung to the tune of "O Tannenbaum," which is also is the tune to "O Maryland, My Maryland" and "Michigan, My Michigan." A tipoff that we're not talking about a unique piece of musical inspiration.

> Thy golden fruit the world outshines
> Florida, my Florida,
> Thy gardens and thy phosphate mines,
> Florida, my Florida,
> Yield their rich store of good supply,
> To still the voice of hunger's cry,—

Yup, sun-kissed land and phosphate mines. "It is recommended for use in daily exercises for the public schools of the state of Florida," the 1913 legislature decreed, proving again that the Florida Legislature's drive to micromanage classroom activity is no recent development.

Gov. David Sholtz, U.S. Sen. Claude Pepper, and others called for something less sing-songy, and in 1935 the legislature passed a resolution recognizing "Swanee River" as the state's song. It was a big hit. Particularly with Sholtz's successor, Fred P. Cone, who was born near the eponymous river and would push for the creation of the Stephen Foster Memorial State Park there.

Gov. Fuller Warren told the story that when campaigning for governor in South Florida, Cone would play records over the public-address system to draw a crowd. But one day in South Florida he found all but one of the records had warped, leaving only a recording of "Swanee River" playable, so he played the tune over and over.

Then Cone's traveling party discovered an amazing thing. The reaction from the audience, composed mostly of former northern residents, was exceedingly favorable. To these converted Yankees, the song carried all the sentiment of Stephen Foster's Old South. And Cone, a picture of simple, rugged honesty, fitted into the scene perfectly . . . from then on, the theme song was "Swanee River," and Cone himself became known as "Old Suwannee."

A great story, and that wily, old silver-tongued Warren had a million of them. Actually, Cone was called "Old Suwannee" because that's where he came from. Still, a great story.

And as in many great semi-true political stories, there's some truth here. Different audiences from different places at different times did come away from the song with different messages. When performed in antebellum days, it was a slow ballad meant to cool the raucous proceedings of the usual traveling minstrel show buffoonery. A number that spoke to the sadness of getting older and sold someplace harsher. Because it fit in nicely, it was part of the show in stage versions of *Uncle Tom's Cabin*. W.E.B. Du Bois in 1903 saw it as one of those rare music hall songs "where the songs of white America have been distinctively influenced by the slave songs or have incorporated whole phrases of Negro melody." The kind of song where "the slave spoke to the world."

After Reconstruction, though, the song didn't seem to be about a slave lamenting separation from the home of his youth anymore. It was heard as the lament of a former slave recalling how good he had it back before the Late Unpleasantness and all that Reconstruction nonsense. Listen to the man, he's still longing for the old plantation just like everyone on the town's Confederate Memorial Day Committee.

And if you were a newcomer from Up North who had no particular attachment to the Lost Cause, you heard something else entirely. An evocation of the sound-stage version of the sleepy Old South you watched at the Bijou. Where New York City songsmiths teamed with Hollywood scriptwriters to evoke simpler days in an idyllic Dixieland. (Cue the banjos!) This was the vision that charmed the skimmer-hatted northern white guys listening to State Sen. Cone's only undamaged record playing on a wind-up gramophone in Dade County.

These days, the song resists any easy cleanup, as successive gubernatorial inaugural committees have discovered. "It's like stepping in manure," Atkins said of efforts to make the song presentable. "It's going to always have that on its feet," and the bluesman had a fragrant point. Why not just ditch it and get a new one?

Because sadly, Florida doesn't figure in a lot of music. We don't have something like "Oklahoma!" a song that demands to be belted out and comes with its own exclamation point. We don't have something exquisitely soulful like "Georgia on My Mind." We don't even have something that would be catchy on an accordion like "Say Hello to Someone from Massachusetts," that state's official state polka. We do have an official state welcome song, "Florida," that was adopted by legislative resolution in 1985 with encouragement from Gov. Bob Graham, who often had a song in his heart. ("Florida is sunshine, waterways and sand / Florida's a special kind of promised land.") It was a more buoyant spare song if anyone wanted to use it, but nobody wanted to use it. Maybe this lack of obvious material is because the state's identity is so fluid; maybe because we contain multitudes, which makes it hard to find something that works for everyone; for whatever reason, we lack a recognizable alternative.

Because no obvious choices presented themselves, the legislature in 2007 authorized a statewide competition for a made-to-order replacement song. The winner, picked from 240 entries with the final round decided by an internet poll, was "Where the Sawgrass Meets the Sky," written by a very nice music teacher from Great Britain but which is objectively kind of awful.

It cannot be performed by a marching band because it's down-tempo; it doesn't have much of beat; and it sounds a good deal like the music that gets played on televangelist cable shows while the 800 number stays on the screen and operators stand by to take your pledge. Forget about it as a singalong. And the lyrics, though inoffensive, are clunky even by state-anthem standards. At least it doesn't celebrate phosphate mines.

Legislation to make this choice official passed House and Senate committees, but support was weak and wavering, particularly in the tradition-bound Senate, where Senate President Jim King fretted that his chamber would look dumb debating "the Swanee River problem" while a budgetary crisis loomed. He expressed that view the same week the Senate debated whether to fine Florida drivers for the offense of hanging plastic replicas of bull testicles from their pickups.

But King, a jovial and resourceful political pro, came up with a compromise to save the measure. "Sawgrass" would become the state anthem—and it does have the earnest, hymnbook-for-modern-youth feel of an anthem—and "Swanee River" would remain the state song, albeit with cleaned-up lyrics specified ("darkies" becomes "dear ones"). Gov. Crist signed the bill on June 30, 2008.

Since then I've never heard the state anthem sung at a public event. Or, for that matter, the state song. Both usually are politely ignored, as official state music so often is.

OFFICIAL STATE TREE

Sabal Palm

Tree

In Praise of the State Treelike Plant

(1) The sabal palmetto palm, which is also known as the cabbage palm, and sometimes as the cabbage palmetto, a tree native to Florida, is hereby designated as the Florida state tree.

(2) Said state tree being now extensively used for commercial purposes, the provisions of this section shall not be construed to limit in any manner said use thereof in business, industry, commerce, for food, or for any other commercial purposes.

—Florida Statute 15.031

AS A CHILD, MY WIFE ATTENDED Sabal Elementary School in Melbourne, named in honor of the official state tree. She can still sing the school song, too. It's to the tune of "Bingo Was His Name-oh"—"S-A-B-A-L, S-A-B-A-L, and Sabal was its name-oh."

And that's the kind of tree a sabal palm is: as familiar and shaggy as a neighborhood dog, something a coastal kid might see every day and sing about with gusto, something that needs only five letters to spell unless you insist on calling it a cabbage palm.

Florida came later to the business of naming a state tree than other states. The legislature took it up in 1949 and characteristically split along regional lines. "Latest word from Tallahassee has it that the House has chosen the majestic royal palm over the less glamorous slash pine backed by a North Florida lobby. Now it appears that the Senate will also go royal, due to the insidious efforts of Miami palmists," wrote *St. Petersburg Times* columnist Dick Bothwell that year.

He quoted the president of the Florida Federation of Garden Clubs, who wrote to the governor saying the royal palm was "no tree for the common people of Florida." The garden clubbers were foursquare for the sabal palm and for the people.

And with good reason. The sabal palm grows everywhere in the state, solving the North Florida–South Florida problem. It's democratic, popping up in trailer courts and fancy beach hotels alike. It's useful; you can eat the heart of palm. It's called "swamp cabbage," because among the things it doesn't taste or look like is cabbage. When cut into logs, the palms are the right size for wharf pilings. Sure, they might rot away quickly, but they'll stay up long enough to give you time to flip the property—which is the Florida Way. And the Y-shaped boot that's left when the frond falls off? That can be decorated with eyes and a nose to make a perfectly cute reindeer head for Christmas decorations. All kinds of uses.

Garden club people know which plants work in a yard, and the clubs were tenacious. As a rule, legislators should heed their advice. The clubs kept advocating for the tree until the measure returned to the legislature in 1953 and finally passed.

Even then, the bill was not without opposition. North Floridians continued their stubborn support for the slash pine. Their number included State Forester C. H. Coulter, "a slash pine supporter to the bitter end," as the Associated Press characterized him. But he and his allies were "bested only when the formidable forces of the Federation of Garden Clubs were arrayed on the side of the sabal. 'I bowed to the inevitable,' said Coulter sadly," the AP reported.

The garden clubs championed their choice of state tree even though, as opponents like Coulter enjoyed pointing out, sabal palms technically are not trees. They're grasses. But most people still call them trees and they look like trees. Nobody says, "Damn, the hurricane took out a thirty-foot stick of grass, and it sure smashed up my rain gutter." Once you start quibbling about taxonomy, there's no telling where it might end.

So, yes, Florida's state tree is not a tree. But isn't that also a Florida thing to do?

Another thing I like about the trees is they don't demand much in the way of care. Sure, the fronds, the stuff around the flowers, and the berrylike seeds fall all over the place, but that's light post-storm cleanup. Easy work.

But I'm here to report that when presented with a mellow, slow-growing, low-maintenance treelike grass, not everybody takes the hint and leaves it alone. In early hurricane season, you'll see people trimming the fronds back to a few sad sprigs in what's called a "hurricane cut." People of Florida: do not inflict this treatment on your state tree. You're hacking at it as if it's a grass. Which it is, but that's no excuse.

It won't help the tree weather the storm, either. It's bad for the tree, and aesthetically, anyone will tell you that it looks silly. It's the poodle-cut of palms. If we're going to maintain the fiction that palm trees are trees, this kind of treatment only gets in the way. Respect your official state treelike plant.

Some state symbols are there because we're afraid we might be losing them—panthers, manatees, gopher tortoises—and others because they're everywhere and define the landscape. The sabal palm is the latter. Which is why I'm fond of their fronds and why even little kids know what they're singing about at Sabal Elementary School.

UNOFFICIAL STATE SPORT

nascar

Sport

The Official State Sport Stalled in the Pits

> The sport of automobile racing is designated
> as the official state sport.

> —Senate Bill 266 (2012)

To live in Daytona Beach and not be into auto racing seems wrong, and I apologize for that all the time. I'm not a racing snob, it's just that cars circling fast look like traffic to me. Having grown up among Florida drivers, I fear getting behind the wheel, which means the whole automotive mystique and love of car lore is beyond me. My previous car was a Saturn, which was an automotive statement about being oblivious to automotive statements.

But it doesn't matter what I think. The fact is My Little Town is known beyond its borders for exactly four things: (1) its role as a Spring Break party town from the late 1980s to early 1990s; (2) as the site of Bike Week; (3) as the place where you can drive your car on the beach, at least at low tide when the sands aren't too soft; and (4) as home to NASCAR, Daytona International Speedway, and the Daytona 500. We tend to celebrate that last thing more than the others. And I, too, cheer it on—only in the abstract and staying well away from the track when the crowds descend.

In 2012 my district's state senator, Evelyn Lynn, introduced legislation to declare auto racing Florida's official state sport. In retrospect, this was a mistake. My area's elected representatives mistook our local culture for the state's culture. A common misapprehension in the official state designation game. The proposal, which seemed natural and obvious to anyone in coastal Volusia County, was greeted in the state capital with a mixture of indifference and derision and a tincture of hostility.

The bill passed the Senate but died in messages at the end of the session, which makes it sound like it got lost in the mail but actually means the House of Representatives didn't feel like taking it up.

North Carolina already had designated stock car racing as its state sport the year before. An action that had hurt local pride, already wounded because that same state stole the NASCAR Hall of Fame out from under us. Who had a speedway first, huh? Where were they racing cars in nineteen goddamn aught three? Where did Bill France the Great and Bill France the Younger, the revered builders of NASCAR, live? In Daytona Beach within the great state of Florida, thank you very much.

But stock car racing, sadly, is a niche sport and remains widely misunderstood. A legislative body full of football fans located within sight of Florida State University wouldn't understand. And a lot of the out-of-town analysis of the sport and its fans carries the faint aroma of condescension, especially when politicians are doing the speaking. When George

W. Bush ran for president, part of his base was labeled "NAS-CAR dads," referring to rural and suburban, white, married, working stiffs who make up much of the race track grandstand crowd. It was a nicer way for political consultants to talk about how to reel in the Bubbas. Bush took this pollster abstraction so literally that he showed up himself at the Daytona 500.

Barack Obama knew NASCAR dads were not part of his base, but he gamely tried to talk up NASCAR as a significant part of American culture. Here's what he said in 2009:

> You know, it's fitting that you've all come here to the White House—the American people's house—because NASCAR is a uniquely American sport. Since its humble beginnings, when moonshiners raced on the sands of Daytona Beach during Prohibition, it's grown into a sport with tens of millions of fans here in America and around the world.

A vivid image and quite a story: revenuers and moonshine runners roaring along the beach at low tide in the dusk. Trading shots with tommy guns. Muzzle-flash lighting the subtropical night and scaring off the sea turtles. Sure, this is a mishmash of misremembered old-time racing stories. But a lot of people conflate the NASCAR founding myth (moonshine runners zooming around country back roads, evading authorities and giving birth to a uniquely southern car culture) and the Daytona International Speedway founding story (beach driving, racing, and speed trials leading to the construction of superspeedways and a racing empire). And sure, none of this had anything remotely to do with Prohibition or the Prohibition Era. Car racing on the beach as organized, regular events started well after alcohol again flowed freely in America. Although as a practical matter, alcohol never stopped flowing in coastal Florida.

Still, it was a distinct pleasure to hear the Leader of the Free World address himself to the history of my hometown and its contribution to national culture. If his research staff made a hash of it—at least they tried, okay? That's more than the Florida Legislature did. The official state sport bill was never reintroduced, but legislators did authorize a NASCAR license plate. A consolation prize. Big whup.

OFFICIAL STATE LITTER CONTROL

Glenn Glitter

Litter Control Symbol

The Short, Happy Life of Glenn Glitter

The litter control symbol and official litter control trademark of the Florida Federation of Garden Clubs, Inc., "Glenn Glitter," is hereby designated as the Florida state litter control symbol.

—Florida Statute 15.041 (1978)

THE MOST MOCKED of our official state symbols is not our official soil, not our never-performed state play (*Cross and Sword*), and not our never-performed official state pageant (*Indian River*) or official state welcome song, but a lowly cartoon insect, Glenn Glitter, Florida's official litter control symbol.

"An actual law mandates that a grinning, bee-like critter named Glenn Glitter be the state's official litter control symbol," wrote a surprised *Miami Herald* feature writer. "There's even a state 'litter control symbol,' under the name of 'Glenn Glitter,' that was approved in 1978, of which nobody has ever heard," noted *St. Petersburg Times* commentator Howard Troxler in 1999. "Remember those zany state legislators who adopted 'Glenn Glitter' as Florida's official litter control symbol?" asked an *Orlando Sentinel* editorial in 1989. And I myself, as a member of the Florida print commentariat, am guilty of going for cheap laughs by evoking Glenn Glitter's official status.

For a brief period in the 1970s you could spot the glitter bug on highway signage, garbage cans, and pamphlets handed out to Florida elementary school students. Glenn Glitter was drawn by a Department of Transportation staffer as a winged insect of some indeterminate kind with an elastic smile and two bent antennae. Sometimes his wings folded down to resemble a yellow safety vest, like the kind issued to public works workers and prisoners doing roadside trash pickup.

The logo was suggested by the Florida Federation of Garden Clubs—a seeming factory for state symbol making, especially members of the Tallahassee chapter, who had come up with the concept. When Gov. Reubin Askew signed the Glenn Glitter Bill into law in 1978, the hope was that Glenn Glitter would become the Smokey Bear of anti-litter efforts.

Many cartoon mascots aspire to Smokey Bear status; few achieve it. Glenn Glitter was kind of gross and crudely drawn. And "Be a glitterbug not a litterbug!" was a slogan that just didn't catch on, even with little kids. Which is the problem with giving official state status to a public service mascot early in its career. Like rock bands, mascots have a high failure and burnout rate. Statutory official state status should be a career achievement award, not something to put on the launch-party press release. You will note that Glenn Glitter's name is not among those immortalized in the Capitol rotunda. As with other discarded celebrities, everybody in town now claims never to have heard of the guy.

And even as political commentators were sniggering at him, Glenn Glitter had already been quietly wiped from the statute books. His name was stricken as one item out of many in a wide-ranging trash-and-litter bill in 1993. Maybe legislators were tired of the ribbing; maybe the logo had run its course; in any case, Glenn Glitter hasn't graced a state garbage can in decades.

Surprisingly, though, you will see his name listed all over the place as Florida's official state litter control symbol. Which shows how hard it is to shake an official state symbol once you've run with one. He's gone but not entirely forgotten.

Mockingbird

Bird

The Mockingbird Will Not Be Mocked, Tree Huggers!

WHEREAS, The Legislature of the State of Florida has thrown the arm of its protecting care around the Mocking Bird by the enactment of suitable legislation and,

WHEREAS, The melody of its music has delighted the heart of residents and visitors to Florida from the days of the rugged pioneer to the present comer, and

WHEREAS, This bird of matchless charm is found throughout our State, therefore

Be It Resolved by the Legislature of the State of Florida:

Section 1. That the Mocking Bird be and it is hereby designated as the State Bird of the State of Florida.

—Senate Concurrent Resolution No. 3 (1927)

FLORIDA'S STATE BIRD CHOICE SURPRISES BIRDERS. In a state teeming with stunning and exotic birdlife, in a state where you might, without much hiking, spot the rosiest of roseate spoonbills, Big Bird–sized great blue herons, poster-colored parrots, and parakeets that had escaped and gone native; in a state where you might encounter the snowiest of snowy egrets standing on your car's hood in a Walmart parking lot, or admire the dignified royal terns sharing the beach with yapping, common gulls, or worry about the way a red-tailed hawk is eyeing your cat; where cartoon-blue scrub jays are as friendly as a Disney-movie bluebird, we have a state bird that is a squawky, average, monochromatic creature found anywhere in the continental United States—the mockingbird. The same state bird claimed by Arkansas, Mississippi, Tennessee, and Texas. A rando yard bird.

It's like making a declaration saying: Nothing to see here, we're just your average yard-bird place. Oh, it's not that bird lovers haven't tried to change this. In 1999, 2000, and 2016, the scrub jay was suggested to the legislature as a more home-team replacement, a bird found only in Florida but sadly in short supply.

And it was precisely the bird's declining numbers (it has been on the federal list of threatened species since 1989) that made it a politically sensitive choice. One that got the attention of development interests alarmed at the prospect of environmentalists using the new state bird as a propaganda tool. They imagined headlines like "County Council OKs Clearcutting State Bird's Habitat for Pump'N'Pay Site."

When this was first debated, however, these concerns remained unstated. Instead of talking about bird habitat and the probable motivations of bird lovers, opponents went negative. Not on the environmentalists. On the scrub jay itself. "They eat the eggs of other birds," huffed Marion Hammer, the powerful National Rifle Association lobbyist and former NRA president, who was vocal in the fight against the scrub jay menace. "That's criminal conduct, that's robbery and murder." She described the bird as "lazy," displaying "a welfare mentality." She almost called it a liberal.

Legislators deadlocked on the issue of avian character, and the bill died that year. But the next year a new version of the bill language addressed developers' concerns: "That the designation of the Florida scrub jay as the official state bird is strictly symbolic and does not require any additional protections or acquisition of habitat," it said. There it was in black and white: just because it's the state bird doesn't mean anyone has to stop killing it or bulldozing places where it lives. Still, that was not enough reassurance.

And it wasn't only development politics in the background. In the deeper background was payback gun politics. Clay Henderson, a pro–scrub jay advocate and Audubon president, had also been a member of the Constitution Revision Commission and as such had called for tougher regulations on gun show sales. Henderson complained that Hammer's role as defender of the mockingbird was no more than "payback from the NRA." Hammer denied this, saying she was lobbying only as a friend of the mockingbird.

Regardless of motives, the aptly named Hammer is not a person to drop an issue once having staked out a position. She opposed a bill in 2009 that would have allowed schoolchildren to pick a state bird (they had the temerity to choose the osprey—kids today!) and resumed her role as friend of the mockingbird and scourge of the scrub jay again in the 2016 legislative session.

But politics aside, there is nothing all that Florida-like about the mockingbird. It's so blah. "I cannot think of a more pathetic choice for one of the most bird-rich states in the nation. What's their state beverage, a half-glass of warm tap water?" asked Nicholas Lund of the Birdist website in 2013. (No, it's a half-glass of warm orange juice.)

I can only guess at the motivations of the 1927 legislature for having done this in the first place. And the Audubon Society can only blame its own St. Petersburg chapter for putting forward the nomination. The chapter's vote "was overwhelmingly for the mockingbird," and not for "the grotesque pelican."

I rather like the grotesque pelican because I'm a coastal dweller and never tire of watching them skim the waves in single file; however, I understand that Louisiana got there first. And in any case, it's also one more bird with no special Florida association. Which is why I always liked the scrub jay proposal and am pleased whenever I see it fluttering back to the Florida Legislature.

Hammer has objected that the scrub jay is only a Central Florida bird, and is not a Florida-wide bird. Not true! It's been spotted in thirty-nine counties—everywhere except the Panhandle and the southern tip of the state. In the county where I live, a scrub jay festival is held every February at the Lyonia Preserve, near Deltona. There's another scrub jay festival in Jonathan Dickinson State Park, and another one at Merritt Island. By contrast, a mockingbird festival wouldn't fly. Who wants a state bird that won't help a festival organizer get things going?

The next time this comes up, count me in favor of giving the scrub jay official state bird status. The best thing about the friendly little blue bird is the way it and its threatened status can slow down progress and thwart runaway sprawl. Even without being the state bird. I have sat though city commission and county council meetings where attorneys had to clear their throats, dust off the old PowerPoint, and explain how they only want to rearrange habitat, not demolish it and pave it completely. The scrub jay is on the right side of a lot of planning and zoning disputes, so the least I can do is be on its side.

And if that causes a problem, there's always the flamingo. It's on our lottery tickets already, and I keep two plastic ones by my front door. Does anyone put a plastic mockingbird in their yard? No, they don't! I yield the floor.

OFFICIAL STATE MOTTO

IN GOD WE TRUST

LIBERTY

2019

In God We Trust

Motto

In God We Trust (All Others Pay Cash)

> "In God We Trust" is hereby designated and declared the official motto of the State of Florida.
>
> —Florida Statute 15.0301

ON FEBRUARY 20, 2018, as five thousand demonstrators, mobilized by the murders at Marjory Stoneman Douglas High School in Parkland, marched on the Florida Capitol demanding gun restrictions, nobody can say the Florida House of Representatives was sitting idle inside. Members were busy passing a resolution declaring pornography a public health threat, and the next day, by a 97–10 vote, they approved legislation ordering schools to display prominently the official state motto, "In God We Trust," at all public schools. The measure did not include money to pay for the display, but it was assumed that Florida's public schools would make do, as Florida's public schools always had.

The representatives were on their feet applauding Kimberly Daniels of Kimberly Daniels Ministries International, author of the book *Spiritual Boot Camp* and Democratic representative from Jacksonville, as she stirred the congregation with denunciations of a secular culture that had lost its bearings. "But the real thing that needs to be addressed are issues of the heart," Daniels declared. She particularly indicted video games. "We cannot put God in a closet when the issues we face are bigger than us," she told the receptive congregation.

Like the Blues Brothers, Florida House members left the service glowing from within and on a mission from God, and thank goodness, it was one that didn't involve talking about guns. It just meant tasking high school shop classes with the job of turning out "In God We Trust" signs. Though in practice many Florida schools got around this by prominently displaying the Florida state seal, since those words are an integral part of the whole state seal package. Nice work-around.

Like many of our state symbols, Florida's state motto is not specific to Florida. It's a generic motto. The original state motto, the one on the state's first flag, was "Let us alone." A popular states' rights slogan in antebellum slave-holding states that discreetly left unspoken exactly what it was that Florida wished to be left alone about. (It was slavery, but hush now.)

This flag did not meet with universal applause. State senators who were Whigs saw it as a dig at them since this was a slogan identified with southern Democrats. The flag itself was kind of a bust, a patchwork vexillological dog's breakfast. It featured five stripes in five colors, a mini United States flag, and a scroll with slogan. Graphic designers were in short supply in those frontier days.

It was flown once and later sent over to the Florida House chamber. No scrap of it survives. In short order, the state moved on to new mottos and slogans.

Surprisingly, the state has gone without a statutorily declared motto for most of its existence. It wasn't until 2006 that Gov. Jeb Bush signed into law a bill recognizing the phrase as the official state motto.

Oh sure, the 1846 state seal had the motto. And when the 1868 legislature cobbled together the present state seal as part of its general rebooting of state government, it decreed that the artwork should be "encircled by the words, 'Great Seal of the State of Florida: In God We Trust.'" But even a child could see that this fell short of being an official state motto. And sure enough, some children did. As part of a class project on state symbols, two ten-year-olds noticed the absence of a formally decreed state motto. And since their parents were lobbyists, an idea was born and made into law. To emphasize the motto further, the legislature passed a bill two years later to give motorists the option of getting license tags that said "In God We Trust" in place of the traditional motto "Sunshine State." Whichever you believe in more.

Personally, I'm unclear about the exact meaning of "In God We Trust." I understand that it is on every scrap of currency in my wallet, along with the declaration that "this note is legal tender for all debts, public and private." When I pass along this twenty-dollar bill, it goes into the hands of another trusting believer. A believer in a future in which others will accept the next twenty bucks printed on paper and believe in the Federal Reserve System and the United States Treasury Department. All ultimately guaranteed by the unseen incorporeal being in whom we trust as well. A lot of layers of trust, not all of which seem necessary for the transaction at hand.

I try not to be a crank about this, but I've grown weary of being dragged into other people's religious observances. On the spectrum of disbelief, I fall somewhere on the Deist/Uni-tarian Universalist/beach-hippy/community-college-adjunct-humanities-instructor spectrum, which is not so rare—we're about a quarter of the population—but in Florida political life this is treated as eccentric, exotic, and troubling. Damn hippies.

Soon after our license-tag choices widened, my daughter and I went to the county tag office to get our license plates. I insisted on the one that said, "Sunshine State," in keeping with my beliefs, but she asked for the new design that said, "In God We Trust."

"Why did you get that one?" I asked.

"Because it would annoy you," she chirped.

I denied this. "I'm not annoyed, I'm just not sure that's someone you should be trusting too much," I said. Similar words were uttered about the last guy she dated.

When I grew up in Central Florida in the 1960s and 1970s, it's not as though the people around me didn't try to put me on a stronger spiritual path. I went to Mass, attended immer-sion baptisms, and listened to the local AM radio station's black gospel music hour because it rocked out and made me feel good. Helpful teachers at my public elementary school handed out copies of the New Testament at Eastertime. I was taught in junior high school science class that this evolu-tion stuff was all hooey. ("Like can only come from like!" my teacher declared to anyone who asked too many questions, as though she had discovered the one big flaw in evolutionary theory that nobody talks about.) I started my higher educa-tion at what was a Baptist-affiliated college where upperclass-men practiced their developing ability to witness to the lost on their unsuspecting classmates.

As a reporter, I dutifully bow my head in public prayers during planning board meetings, city commission workshops, county council sessions, political rallies, legislative session starts, fundraising dinners, service club luncheons, and athletic events. Except for athletes, nobody participates in governmental and public event prayer more than reporters. Yet somehow we are seldom recognized as moral exemplars.

I do this often enough that I consider myself an expert in the art. I prefer my prayers inclusive, like the ones the late Rev. Hal Marchman used to give. Marchman was a Baptist minister who for decades ended prayers at all major NASCAR races with the shouted benediction: "Shalom and amen!" He prayed for everybody, ecumenically, with cheerful gusto, and always with an awareness the clock was ticking. The way it should be done. A real pro. I miss him.

More usual, though, are city commissioners who give meandering sermonettes evoking the Trinity and Jesus's part of it, regardless of audience makeup. I realize they do this with the clueless offense given by people who assume everyone else is just like them. They aren't trying to announce: "This is no town, county or state for you heathens, heretics, and infidels out there! Depart this sanctified chamber of government!" Though the more sensitive among us might walk away with that impression.

These exercises sometimes impart surprisingly specific theology about the Trinity, divine will, angels, the divine sanction of secular authority, God's Plan, even the coming End Days. Historically, people have killed each other over these distinctions, yet I get dragged into them for being at a city commission meeting called to decide zoning variances. Why?

Worse still are the prayers at the Florida Legislature, where a minister will depict God and His angels as merely one more pressure group ready to trade favors in exchange for the right legislative consideration. God will shower His blessings upon a people who support House Bill 839 as amended by committee.

With this rich spiritual background, I should be a better person than I am. Mama tried. Well, actually she didn't. Her exact theological position is a matter of family debate, but she didn't have much use for organized religion. It wasn't a big thing with her. She was polite to a fault and never wanted to rain on, or even cloud, anyone's parade. She taught us to hear out people's beliefs carefully and only afterward, within a private setting, wonder at the goofy stuff some people are putting out there.

My daughter is more spiritual than either of us and drove her car with Florida's "In God We Trust" plate trustingly to California and points beyond. Her twin brother, however, believes in an impersonal universe that crushes people indifferently. He's an economist.

So yes, I suppose my daughter was right that bolting an "In God We Trust" plate on her car would, slowly and over time, kind of grate on me. Since then, like many Florida drivers, I have traded in my standard-issue Sunshine State tag for a specialty plate, one that raises money for bicycle safety. It says, "Share the Road." Which, spiritually and metaphorically, wouldn't be a bad official motto for the state in general. But that awaits a future class project.

Seal

Not a Great Seal, but Not for Lack of Trying

The great seal of the state shall be of the size of the American silver dollar, having in the center thereof a view of the sun's rays over a highland in the distance, a sabal palmetto palm tree, a steamboat on water, and an Indian female scattering flowers in the foreground, encircled by the words "Great Seal of the State of Florida: In God We Trust."

—Florida Statute 15.03

FLORIDA'S GREAT SEAL, well, it ain't so great. It used to be worse, so at least it's evolving. A good seal, not a great seal.

In most states, people go about their lives unaware of the great seal in their area. In Flagler County, where my wife works, people are always surprised to learn that the county's great seal is a potato inside a circle. Just a clip-art potato, that's it. But unlike Flagler County, Florida puts its great seal right in the middle of the state flag for all to see. You can't avoid it.

Looked at from beneath an elementary school flagpole, the state seal looks like a plate of scrambled eggs. There are a lot of elements in it, and it's hard to pick out the particulars from ground level. A busy emblem is always a sign of committee work. The seal has the aesthetics of a cigar box lid.

Let's list the elements: A native woman spreading flower blossoms, a palm tree, steamship, the sun spreading its rays, a river, scattered palmettos, and the slogan "In God We Trust." As I said, a lot is happening here. It's like those paper placemats you sometimes see in diners that picture all the state attractions spread over a Florida map with leaping dolphins and marlins, menacing alligators, fiery rocket launches, waving water skiers, Bok Tower, and racing cars beneath a smiling sun wearing Ray-Bans.

But beach life and rockets were all in the future when this was sketched out. The seal was a rush job in 1868, and the newly reconstituted Florida Legislature that voted for it had bigger concerns. Like finding new and more creative ways to get Gov. Harrison Reed to leave town. (The legislature impeached him four times, but he served out his term.)

Historian T. Frederick Davis wrote a short but withering critique of the state's seal in 1924 for the *Florida Historical Quarterly*. The old, perfectly adequate seal, he said, had been "discarded by a legislature composed principally of people who had not even a bona fide residence here. Therefore, it is not surprising that the seal they provided in its place, our present seal, should have historical inaccuracies, one of which is positively ridiculous."

Davis was down on the whole Reconstruction project ("a bitter mockery to the Southern people") and saw this as just one more damn thing it got wrong. Still, it's hard to argue with him here. The biggest howler he pointed out was the mountains. It's amazing how many artists of Florida in the nineteenth century and before felt a need to include a mountain or two when depicting the place. The artists had a point. Our landscape does cry out for mountains. Just one, in addition to Space Mountain, would be a nice thing to have. Not even a big one, just something extra for the tourists. Instead, we make do with "I climbed Mount Dora" T-shirts.

The Native American woman in the foreground was dressed like a cigar-store kind of Indian, sort of like someone from a Plains tribe. ("An unclassified savage," Davis complained.) In later iterations of the seal, she looks an extra from the John Wayne movie *Fort Apache*.

"The Seminole Indians did not wear the head-dress illustrated in our seal. It was characteristic of tribes farther north and those of the West, and it was an insignia of distinction for the head-men and warriors exclusively. Their women did not wear it," Davis wrote. And again, I can't argue.

Renderings of the old seal still grace courthouses around the state and even the frieze on the pediment of the old Capitol Building, where they have confused viewers and amused commentators for more than century. Cigar-store-Indian-and-mountain seals still adorn the courthouse rotunda where I live. They are inlaid in the wall, so there's nothing to be done about them. I always enjoy pointing them out to newcomers. "That's Mount Dora in the background," I tell them.

Architecture isn't easy to fix, but a seal is. As long as you keep all the legislatively prescribed elements in place, any secretary of state is allowed to touch things up, and they have. At some point the mountains were changed to orange groves and later the orange groves disappeared too, as they so often do once developers arrive in town. R. A. Gray, who was secretary of state for ages, from 1930 to 1961, altered the unclassified savage's dress so she'd show less leg, and he made the decoration on her shoulder bag look more like a Christian-style cross, so we'd know she's a Christian and not an animist throwing flowers around as part of some heathen rite.

The legislature in 1970 changed the statute so that the palm tree would be the official state tree, the sabal palm, and not a cocoa palm, which is a South Florida plant. I'm not saying this was another example of the legislature's traditional hostility toward South Florida, but there you have it. Fortunately, all the secretary of state had to do as keeper of the seal was erase the coconuts, and everything would look statutorily correct. No biggie.

Tired of lame jokes about the odd elements in the state seal—(even the steamboat looked wrong; was it sinking?)—Secretary of State George Firestone secretly gave state researchers the task of redesigning things. Get the native woman to look more like a Florida Seminole native woman, make the ship more seaworthy, make the palm look more sabal-like, emphasize the sun's rays, make the flowers look more like hibiscus and less like a generic cartoon-strip flower, and trim the palmetto brushes while you're at it. Still a bustling scene that looks like the breakfast special when seen on a flagpole, but one that is, in its specifics, more local, less laughable.

Firestone rolled it all out in 1985 to applause. ("At last, seal looks like Florida," editorialized the *Miami Herald*.) The new seal and the flags displaying it popped up everywhere in no time. It's been in use ever since.

No alligator, though. The scene demands an alligator. The secretary of state has the power to fix this and should get on it. State symbolism in Florida is a job that knows no rest.

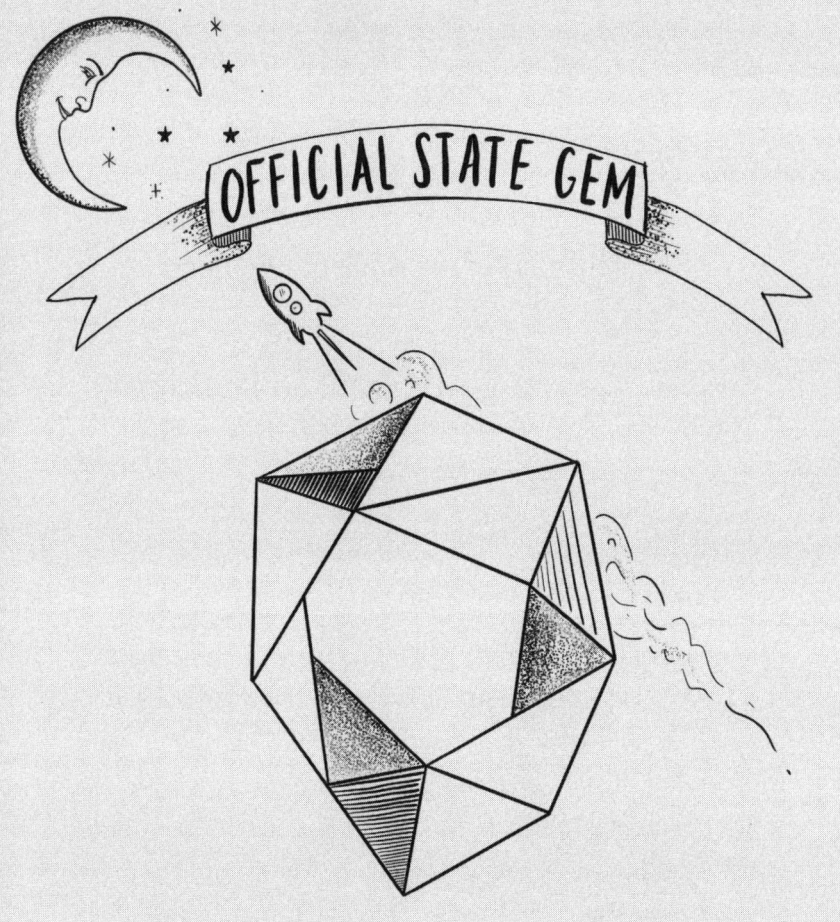

OFFICIAL STATE GEM

Moonstone

Gem

The Talisman of the Ancient Engineers

The moonstone, a transparent or translucent feldspar of pearly
or opaline luster, is hereby designated the Florida state gem.

—Florida Statute 15.034

THE OFFICIAL STATE GEM of Florida is the moonstone. Not
because you can dig one up anywhere in Florida except at an
estate sale; not because it has some association with some
obscure bit of state lore; but because the year was 1970 and
rockets launched from right here at Kennedy Space Center
were sending astronauts to the moon. The future was here!
"Gateway to Discovery," as the state's commemorative quarter would reiterate thirty years later.

If you want to go to the moon, well then, you'll need to
pass through Florida first, won't you? This was more of an aspirational state symbol. Boosters told us the day was dawning
when going to the moon would be a thing, a state industry,
and Florida was the logical jumping-off spot.

What the legislature didn't understand, or maybe didn't
want to think about, was that after American astronauts ar-

rived on the moon, nobody had a good idea for the next act. The great manned space effort demobilized breathtakingly fast. NASA and private industry laid off thousands of space workers, and Central Florida experienced its first space-biz recession.

Yet I do understand the optimism behind the moonstone in the 1970 session, even if it was misguided. I inherited that optimism.

I was able to enjoy growing up in a less-developed 1960s Florida because my dad was called in to work on the Apollo project. There is a straight line from President John F. Kennedy telling a 1961 joint session of Congress the nation should adopt the goal "before this decade is out, of landing a man on the moon and returning him safely to the Earth," and me rolling out of the back of a green Rambler American station wagon to grab free orange juice at the Florida welcome station off U.S. Highway 1 in 1962.

My dad latched on to the Florida Dream fast. Growing up in a gritty coal-mining town and then getting a look at the bigger, sunnier world in the Navy while stationed in California made Florida feel like precisely the right place. He had ended up in Upstate New York working for General Electric soon after discharge, which seemed wrong, and just the winter before had wrenched his back shoveling snow. He jumped at the chance to head to the Sunbelt.

October 1962 was not a popular month for becoming a new Floridian. The Cuban Missile Crisis created overheated speculation on the best spot for a medium-range nuclear missile strike, and Florida seemed as good a guess as any. That's why, once I got into the public school system, I was marched single file into the Ortona Elementary School cafetorium to huddle under a table for civil defense drills. Because a good, solid pine table with hardened dots of gum beneath was just the thing to protect you from a nuclear blast. (But be sure to cover and close your eyes so you won't be blinded by the flash.) An exercise that I suspect turned me into something of a lifelong peacenik.

Dad was not slowed by such loose talk. A 1960s design engineer was conditioned to believe in the future. That there would be one, and once it got here, that it would be cooler than now. It might not be the Carousel of Progress that was promised (hey, where's the monorail?), but it would be something at least as good once the unavoidable technical glitches were addressed and the right government funding was secured. Anyway, a Gateway to Discovery had been contracted for, and it would need launch and checkout systems of a kind that didn't yet exist. Bringing this together would require a lot of tools, but a snow shovel would not be among them. Get into the car, kids!

We were part of a new tech sector that swept into Central Florida all at once. My town never had a technological middle class, and it got one in the space of a few months. A group that arrived; fell in love with the beaches; was appalled by the school system; was surprised at the lack of city services; was confused by the kind of racial segregation imposed by the blunt force of law rather than by custom and practice; and was delighted to settle into homes without furnaces that on their lighted doorbells displayed Florida Power and Light's Gold Medallion Home symbol, testifying to the fact that we were living better electrically. The Moonstone Wave had arrived.

The Moonstone Wave was felt most forcefully in Brevard

County, where space program–related employment soon reached 22 percent of the workforce. The county doubled in size over the 1960s. But space biz also overflowed into Volusia County, where I landed, and lapped into Orange County.

Once unpacked, Dad took off exploring our exotic surroundings and began driving the family to every attraction in easy reach: Marineland, DeLeon Springs, Silver Springs, Weeki Wachee, Cypress Gardens, the Citrus Tower, Six-Gun Territory, Sea Zoo, multiple alligator farms, jungle cruises, and parrot farms that would soon fold because Disney World would open and the Interstate Highway System bypassed them. As he got the lie of the land, Dad realized this was mere tourist stuff. He bought a used boat and hit the water. And when fishing got boring, he took up scuba diving to go deeper. Along the way we drove out on beach roads in our Volkswagen beetle (a lightweight car with high clearance, perfect for beach paths) and pulled off the parkways carrying transistor radios—radios almost the size of cigarette packs!—to listen to the countdown and watch launches open-mouthed.

This immersion in Florida Roadside Attractions Land, along with dipping into every spring within a six-county area at an impressionable age, led me to a lifetime as a Floridaologist. At heart, I still see the state as one big roadside attraction crawling with monkeys and alligators and perfumed with flowers the size of dinner plates. Dad, too, embraced the whole Florida thing and rejected any promotion or project that would force us to move.

But even as legislators rhapsodized about the moonstone and the future for which it was a talisman, the layoffs had started at Kennedy Space Center and rippled beyond. Two years after the moonstone was named the official state gem, the last moon mission landed. The next year, a recession hit, and the space budget was slashed.

The recession and budget cuts hit the Moonstone Wave hard. The engineers who could do so shifted their skills and recomposed their resumes, usually with national defense in mind. Some who were determined to stay in Florida retired early or changed careers. In Florida a real estate license is always Plan B.

The Martin Marietta Corporation bought General Electric's aerospace division in 1992 and closed its Daytona Beach facility the next year. Volusia County dropped out of the space economy except for a few workers who commuted to Brevard and scattered contractors. My dad took early retirement and stayed put. Because where would you retire if you already lived in Florida, owned a boat, and had air tanks in the garage?

My dad is now in his late eighties. The Moonstone Wave as a group is getting old, but I run into them sometimes. You'd be surprised how many stayed in Florida. Some hung on the whole time, some chased jobs into other states yet found their way back into town. I refer to them collectively as the Ancient Engineers. They took up two pews at my mother's funeral.

The Moonstone Wave undoubtedly changed the state. I think for the better, even though there was no lack of local pushback and resentment. (Popular 1970s pickup truck bumper sticker: "I don't care how you did it Up North!") We celebrate that remarkable time, and yet Florida never did turn into the promised California-style tech incubator. Not for lack of trying, but stuff happened. The Gateway to Discovery has a way of slamming shut in the wind from time to time.

I'm struck by the way the other children of the Ancient Engineers tend to visit them from out of state. There just wasn't much for them here in a tourism-and-lawn-service economy. I suspect Florida's legendary lack of commitment to education was probably a factor, too. "We're cheap, and we're proud of it" (*Humiles sumus et quoque superbi*) was the motto State University System Chancellor Charlie Reed suggested for Florida education as he, too, got ready to decamp for California in 1997.

But a few children of the Moonstone Wave stuck around. You can spot them now that launches have resumed courtesy of private space companies. Where I live, the best place to see a Falcon launch is atop one of the high-rise bridges spanning the Intracoastal Waterway. Teachers don't send kids out into school frontyards single-file to look skyward anymore, and launches don't empty offices into parking lots the way they did in the Moonstone Wave era. But smatterings of space enthusiasts show up on the bridges all the time. Even for minor weather satellite launches. You can get smartphone apps to alert you when a rocket is about to go off, which is handy because launch schedules don't always make the newspapers the way they did in the Moonstone Wave era.

I look around at each gathering and usually there are kids, there are children of the Moonstone Wave era who grew up considering spaceflight important and a sign that we're living in the future, and only once in a while, I think I've spotted one of the thinning number of Ancient Engineers.

I was brought up technologically hopeful and never shook

it despite the aerospace recession of the 1970s, the *Challenger* and *Columbia* disasters, the empty sky at the end of the space shuttle program, the ongoing lack of consensus on where to go next, and the baffling emergence of moonwalk denialists who don't believe we were ever the kind of society that could do something like that.

I crane my neck hoping the latest vapor trail breaks through the clouds and hope to spot the staging, too, which you can only do when the sky is exceptionally clear and the rocket exceptionally big. And I make a wish upon a moonstone for bigger fireworks to come.

Afterword

A bill to be entitled An Act to Establish the Official State Footwear and Reform Certain State Symbols:

1 WHEREAS, the flip-flop is emblematic of stylish
2 insouciance and the Florida mindset of being perpetu-
3 ally on vacation, and
4 WHEREAS, these simple sandals, based on the
5 Japanese *zori,* have proven versatile, economical, and
6 uniquely adapted to Florida's climate and conditions,
7 and
8 WHEREAS, for the purpose of this statute, a flip-
9 flop is defined as a simple sandal, lacking a back
10 strap, made of synthetic materials and secured with
11 a Y-shaped strap anchored in front with material that
12 is meant to slip between the hallux, or big toe, and
13 second toe, and
14 WHEREAS, this beloved footwear has found favor
15 in all regions of Florida but especially on the coasts,
16 and
17 WHEREAS, certain revisions to Chapter 15, Florida
18 Statutes, are called for.

19 | THEREFORE, Be It Enacted by the Legislature of the
20 | State of Florida:

21 |

22 | Florida Statute 15.0528 is created, reading as
23 | follows:

24 |

25 | Section 1: The sandal known as the flip-flop is the
26 | official State footwear of the State of Florida.

27 | Section 2: For the purposes of signs and rules that
28 | say, "No shirt, no shoes, no service," or like prohibi-
29 | tions, the flip-flop is to be defined as a shoe.

30 | Section 3: The theft of flip-flops left unattended on a
31 | public beach or public beach walkway is a third-degree
32 | felony, even if they looked like the ones you said you
33 | lost, because who do you think you're fooling?

34 | Section 4: This takes effect on the first sunny day
35 | after being signed into law.

36 | Section 5: The barking tree frog is designated as the
37 | official state amphibian while we're at it. They sound
38 | so cool.

39 | Section 6: The Eocene heart urchin is the official
40 | state fossil of the State of Florida.

41 | Section 7: Chapter 15.0327, Florida Statutes, is
42 | hereby repealed and Florida will skip the whole official
43 | state song thing for now.

44 | Section 8: The scrub jay is the official state bird of
45 | the State of Florida.

Acknowledgments

Thanks to Meredith Morris-Babb of the University Press of Florida for suggesting this topic and being a good sport about my Florida Man attitude toward deadlines. And to my employers at the *Daytona Beach News-Journal,* including editor Pat Rice, for being not only tolerant of outside projects but encouraging.

This book has benefitted greatly from the editing skills and suggestions from my patient and sharp-eyed wife, Cindi Lane, and from my daughter, Rachel Inez Marshall. Thanks, too, to the talented Erica Group Kiel, who didn't think the request for drawings of pies and a litter-control mascot was at all strange. And to Kermit's Key West Key Lime Shoppe for the pie recipe and background about their craft.

Notes

KEY LIME PIE: PIE WEDGE OR CANDY-COLORED WEDGE ISSUE?

The first try came in 1988: Marilyn Weeks, "Senate May Toss Out Key Lime Pie Bill," *Sun-Sentinel,* April 27, 1988.

. . . *she had to settle for half a slice*: Doris Quan, "Whipping Up Proof of Pie's Eminence," *Miami Herald,* April 3, 1994.

. . . *the pink flamingos of Florida food*: "Key Lime Pies and Pink Flamingos?" *Orlando Sentinel,* March 24, 2006; House Resolution 139, 113th Congress, First Session.

. . . *State Rep. Dwight Stansel, argued against*: Ashley Fantz, "Out of the Oven," *Miami Herald,* March 2, 2006.

. . . *researchers made another claim*: "Senate Staff Analysis and Economic Impact Statement," archive.flsenate.gov/data/session/2006/Senate/bills/analysis/pdf/2006s0676.go.pdf.

. . . *was not patented*: https://patents.google.com/patent/US15553A/en.

. . . *Aunt Sally*: For example, David Sloan, *The Key Lime Pie Cookbook* (Phantom Press, 2013), 33–34, and Molly O'Neill, "The Curious Case of Key Lime Pie," *Epicurious,* http://www.epicurious.com/archive/seasonalcooking/winter/key-lime-pie.

. . . The WPA Guide to Florida *warned*: Federal Writers' Project, *WPA Guide to Florida,* 196.

. . . Borden's Evaporated Milk Book of Recipes: Borden's Condensed Milk Company, *Borden's Evaporated Milk Book of Recipes* (1919).

... *"Magic Lemon Meringue Pie"*: Borden's Condensed Milk Company, *World's Easiest Recipes for the Automatic Refrigerator* (1935), 12.

By 1940 Monroe Boston Strause: Monroe Boston Strause, "Florida Key Lime Pie," *School and College Cafeteria* 4 (1940): 20.

... A Date with a Dish: Freda De Knight, *A Date with a Dish: A Cook Book of American Negro Recipes* (Hermitage Press, 1948), 71.

... *the Key West Women's Club published*: Key West Woman's Club, *Key West Cook Book*, 215.

... *is popular Florida fare*: "Key Lime Pie Is Popular Florida Fare," *Miami Herald*, November 13, 1949.

... *the earliest mention in the* New York Times: P. D. Converse, "Eating Well on the Trip," *New York Times*, July 14, 1940.

... *a 1951* LIFE *photo feature*: "Season in the Sun," *LIFE*, April 9, 1951, 59.

... *an inviting appearance*: Diane P. Rowell, "Key West Visitor Asks Lime Pie Recipe," *St. Petersburg Times*, March 24, 1953.

... *activist Stetson Kennedy*: Kennedy, *Grits and Grunts*, 146.

... *unlawful to use the term*: *Journal of the House*, May 20, 1965, 858.

... *in Nora Ephron's novel*: Ephron, *Heartburn*, 166.

... *in the* Joy of Cooking: Irma Rombauer and Marion Rombauer Becker, *Joy of Cooking* (New York: Bobbs-Merrill Company, 1975), 657.

SLOGAN: WELCOME TO THE SUNSHINE—NOT THE ALLIGATOR—STATE

The city slogan's origins date to sometime in the 1910s: John Carter, "Beach's Biggest Fan Left 'Famous' Legacy," *Daytona Beach News-Journal*, December 28, 1999. I have found the phrase in advertising going back to 1915.

... The Rainbow Book of American Folk Tales and Legends: Maria Leach, *The Rainbow Book of American Folk Tales and Legends* (World Publishing Company, 1958), 79.

"Florida has always been called the Sunshine state": Carita Doggett, *Florida, Empire of the Sun: A Description of the Living Advantages of Florida Cities, the Pleasures, Recreations and Resort Facilities Now*

Available to Visitors and Prospective Residents (Florida State Hotel Commission, 1930), 8.

. . . *State Sen. Joseph Johnston*: Andrew Meacham, "Epilogue: Joseph Johnston, Father of Sunshine State License Plate," *St. Petersburg Times*, May 28, 2009.

REPTILE: THE FIERCEST STATE SYMBOL IN THE WHOLE SWAMP

Example headline: Samantha Putterman, "'Y'all got beer still?' Florida Man Runs around Store Chasing Customer with Live Alligator," *Bradenton Herald*, July 30, 2018, and Amy L. Edwards, "He Was Naked, on Crack and in Alligator's Mouth—Florida Man's Ordeal," *Seattle Times*, December 1, 2006.

. . . *"the subtle, greedy alligator"*: Bartram and Van Doren, *Travels of William Bartram*, 115.

. . . *substituting "Jim Smith"*: Staff and wire report, "His Venom Is Showing," *Sun-Sentinel*, April 28, 1987.

Martinez signed the bill: "Official State Reptile Pose," *Orlando Sentinel*, May 12, 1987.

. . . *unprovoked alligator attacks*: Florida Fish and Wildlife Conservation Commission, "Alligator Bites on People in Florida," http://my fwc.com/media/1716/alligator-gatorbites.pdf; Daniel Figueroa IV, "Alligator Attacks Are on the Rise in Florida. Thank Humans, Scientists Say," *Tampa Bay Times*, August 23, 2018.

FRUIT: THE WHOLE ORANGE GETS ITS DUE

. . . *had neither oranges nor a city there*: Mark Lane, "Orange City Dwellers Won't Be Blue," *Daytona Beach News-Journal*, September 27, 2013.

. . . *hopeful for the future*: Carse and Foss, *Florida*, 77.

To persons of foresight and capital: Ibid.

. . . *attempt to take care of an orange grove*: Jesse DeWitt Spitzer, "Winter Glimpses of Florida." *Frank Leslie's Popular Monthly* 31, no. 2 (February 1891): 216–24.

The orange fever years: Stronge, *The Sunshine Economy*, 57.

Most people already think: Michon Ashmore, "Deliberation Includes Less-Important Matters," *Tampa Tribune*, March 6, 2005.

Gov. Jeb Bush signed the bill: Richard Dymond, "Kids See the Fruit of Their Labor," *Bradenton Herald*, May 21, 2005.

FOSSIL: PAIN IN MY EOCENE HEART

. . . (the Dixie Cup Clary Local Control Act): Mark Schlueb, "New Law Lets Dogs Dine Outside at Restaurants," *Sun-Sentinel*, June 3, 2006; *Florida Statutes* 509.233 (2006).

But he withdrew the amendment: Mark Harper, "Designation Like Pie in the Face of Senate," *Daytona Beach News-Journal*, April 6, 2006.

The Eocene epoch: For a nice overview see Jonathan Bryan, Thomas Scott, and Guy Means, *Roadside Geology of Florida* (Mountain Press, 2008), 32–35.

Index of Forbidden Phrases: Frank Cerabino, "10 Ways for Officials to Not Say 'Climate Change,'" *Palm Beach Post*, March 25, 2015.

"I'm not a scientist": Sean Sullivan, "Marco Rubio: Earth's Age 'One of the Great Mysteries,'" *Washington Post*, November 19, 2012.

MARINE MAMMAL: WELCOME TO THE LAND OF THE MANATEE MAILBOXES

. . . all added to the official state menagerie: 1975 *Journal of General Legislation*, 197.

Among Florida's 122 specialty license plates: https://www.flhsmv.gov/specialtytags/tagsales.pdf.

. . . six of them for every living manatee: This assumes a manatee population of about 8,000. See Craig Pittman, "New Manatee Population Estimate Hits 7,000 to 10,000 but More than 700 Have Died This Year," *Tampa Bay Times*, December 19, 2018. For difficulties in determining manatee count see Pittman, *Manatee Insanity*, chapter 15, passim.

Boaters killed 119 manatees: Craig Pittman, "Manatee Death Toll: 804," *Tampa Bay Times*, December 31, 2018.

Soil: Myakka Fine Sand, and a Fine Sand It Is

"Mr. Myakka": Charlie Patton, "He's Got All the Dirt on Soil; Advocate Retires from Earthy Job," *Florida Times-Union*, September 15, 2003. See also Watts and Yamataki, "History of Establishing a State Soil," 44–50.

. . . *he delivered a speech*: Carl Hiaasen, "It's Official: Florida's Soil Isn't Just Dirt," *Miami Herald*, June 21, 1989.

. . . *editorial pages and newspaper columnists giggled*: "If Soil Is Due Honor, Make It Muck," *Sun-Sentinel*, April 28, 1988; Bob Morris, "Now for Something Completely Different," *Orlando Sentinel*, January 18, 1988.

. . . *no joke*: Editorial reprinted in Watts and Yamataki, "History of Establishing a State Soil," 49.

Florida Day: Ponce de Leon Schlepped Here!

. . . *unveiling of the statue*: Mark Lane, "Ponce Schemes—Where's Our Statue?" *Daytona Beach News-Journal*, April 4, 2013.

. . . *renamed by legislative memorial*: *Decisions of the United States Geographic Board, June 1923–June 1927: Second Supplement to the Fifth Report*, Government Office (1927), 32.

Maritime historian Samuel Eliot Morison: Morison, *The European Discovery of America*, 502.

. . . *local historians already had been running*: Gold, *History of Volusia County*, 7.

Florian Mann: Mann, *The Story of Ponce de Leon.*

. . . *a blonde in a one-piece*: Francis P. Johnson, "Dorothy Berner holding the hand of the Ponce De Leon statue—DeLeon Springs, Fla." (1954), black and white photo print, State Archives of Florida, Florida Memory, https://www.floridamemory.com/items/show/71987.

. . . *declared that our discoverer arrived at a site "28 degrees north"*: Douglas T. Peck, "Reconstruction and Analysis of the 1513 Discovery Voyage of Juan Ponce de Leon." *Florida Historical Quarterly*, 71, no. 2 (October 1992): 146.

. . . *as late as the 1950s*: Bob Desiderio, "Christmas Day Is Christmas Day, as Far as Holiday Observances Go," *Daytona Beach News-Journal*, November 1, 2004.

. . . *as far back as 1915*: "April the Twenty-sixth," *Daytona Daily News*, April 26, 1915.

. . . *made Confederate Memorial Day a legal holiday*: www.flsenate.gov/Session/Bill/2018/224/Analyses/2018s00224.ca.PDF.

. . . *a major project of the United Daughters of the Confederacy*: Cox, *Dixie's Daughters*.

. . . *quietly shunted the whole thing off*: Date, *Jeb*, 195.

Sen. Lauren Book: Mark Lane, "Dealing with Confederate Past Is No Holiday," *Daytona Beach News-Journal*, February 11, 2018.

. . . *worth the squeeze*: Dan Sweeney, "Senate Panel Approves Ending Confederate State Holidays," *Sun-Sentinel*, February 7, 2018.

. . . *cultural genocide*: Ibid.

Confederate Flag anti-desecration: Florida Statutes 256.051, "Improper use or mutilation of state or Confederate flag or emblem prohibited."

STATE DAY: FLORIDA STATEHOOD DAY ORATION

"The God of Nature made the Suwannee River": Cash and Dodd, *Florida Becomes a State*, 370.

Bankers, duelists, and "persons convicted": Florida Constitution of 1838, article VI, secs. 3–5.

. . . *several victory margins*: Cash and Dodd, *Florida Becomes a State*, 376–77.

. . . *not a bunch of details*: Ibid., 70, 378.

From what was finally divulged: Ibid., 70.

PLAY: MEN IN TIGHTS WITH CROSS AND SWORD

The play hasn't been performed since 1996: Rick De Yampert, "Amped at the Amphitheatre," *Daytona Beach News-Journal*, August 21, 2008; "Cross and Sword," http://www.lostparks.com/crossandsword.html.

... listed 47 actors: Cross and Sword program, P. K. Yonge Library of
Florida History, University of Florida, Gainesville.

Matanzas High School: Mark Lane, "Old Battle, New School Odd Mix,"
Daytona Beach News-Journal, April 3, 2005.

... an audience of fewer than 10,000: Christian H. Moe, Scott J. Parker,
and George McCalmon, Creating Historical Drama (Southern Illi-
nois University Press, 2005), 30.

... the dreamers walked this land: Green, Cross and Sword.

Song: Florida's Official Ol' Plantation Song

When Charlie Crist was inaugurated: Lloyd Dunkelberger, "Crist
Spurns 'Old Folks' for New Tune at Event," Sarasota Herald-Tribune,
January 3, 2007, 8A.

... wasn't exactly the inclusive message: Crist and Henican, The Party's
Over.

The song was reworded: "Jeb Bush Takes Oath in Chill," Sarasota Herald-Tribune, January 6, 1999; Roberts, Dream State, 97.

... even in instrumental form: John Oliver, "Last Week Tonight," broad-
cast September 9, 2018.

"Florida, My Florida": House Concurrent Resolution no. 24 (1913).
Journal of the House of Representatives of the Session of 1913, 1376–77.

Fred P. Cone, who was born: Nelson, How the New Deal Built Florida
Tourism, 162.

Gov. Fuller Warren told the story: Warren and Morris, How to Win in
Politics, 167–68.

... stage versions of Uncle Tom's Cabin: Emerson, Doo-dah! 199–200.

W.E.B. Du Bois: Du Bois, The Souls of Black Folk, 123.

"It's like stepping in manure": Gretchen Parker, "Racist Screed or Enlightened Work? State Song Stirs Up Folks at Home," Tampa Tribune, January 20, 2007.

... was adopted by legislative resolution: HCR 1430, Journal of the House
of Representatives, May 29, 1985, 850.

... authorized a statewide competition: Mark Lane, "State Song Pick
Needs Do-Over," Daytona Beach News-Journal, March 16, 2008.

... came up with a compromise: Linda Kleindienst, "Senate Cleans Up

Lyrics of State Song—'Swanee River' May Stay, Anthem Added,"
Sun-Sentinel, April 25, 2008; *Florida Statutes* 15.0326.

TREE: IN PRAISE OF THE STATE TREELIKE PLANT

Latest word from Tallahassee: Dick Bothwell, "Go Ahead Lawmakers—
Pick a State Tree, Any State Tree," *St. Petersburg Times*, April 29,
1949.

State Forester C. H. Coulter: Associated Press, "State Tree, Sabal Palm,
Is Useful," *St. Petersburg Times*, June 23, 1953.

SPORT: THE OFFICIAL STATE SPORT STALLED IN THE PITS

In 2012, my district's state senator: Derek Catron, "Auto Racing Continues Drive to Become Official State Sport," *Daytona Beach News-
Journal*, February 23, 2012.

Barack Obama knew: Barack Obama, "Remarks by the President
Honoring 2008 NASCAR Sprint Cup Champion Jimmie Johnson," August 19, 2009, https://obamawhitehouse.archives.gov/
realitycheck/the_press_office/Remarks-by-the-President-honoring-
2008-NASCAR-Sprint-Cup-Champion-Jimmie-Johnson.

LITTER CONTROL SYMBOL: THE SHORT, HAPPY LIFE OF GLENN GLITTER

An actual law mandates: Mary Voboril, "Florida Pride: It's the law," *Mi-
ami Herald*, November 4, 1986, 1B; Howard Troxler, "Florida Must
Coin an Image Worth a Flip," *St. Petersburg Times*, June 16, 1999;
"Earth to Tallahassee! Over!" *Orlando Sentinel*, April 21, 1989.

The logo was suggested: Linda H. Yates and Libby Penrod, "Garden
Club Thrives at 90," *Tallahassee Democrat*, October 13, 2016; Mary
Voboril, "Florida Pride: It's the law," *Miami Herald*, November 4,
1986.

His name was stricken: *Florida Laws* Ch. 93–207.

BIRD: THE MOCKINGBIRD WILL NOT BE MOCKED, TREE HUGGERS!

They eat the eggs of other birds: Craig Pittman, "Efforts to Replace the
Mockingbird as State Bird Run into a Powerful Foe," *St. Petersburg
Times*, September 9, 2009; Lane, *Sandspurs*, 106.

... *addressed developers' concerns*: Lane, *Sandspurs,* 106.

... *"payback from the NRA"*: "After Fuss and Feathers, Mockingbird Still Our Bird," *St. Petersburg Times,* April 9, 1999.

... *a more pathetic choice*: Nicholas Lund, "What State Birds *Should* Be," *Slate,* May 17, 2013, http://www.slate.com/articles/health_and_science/science/2013/05/state_bird_improvements_replace_cardinals_and_robins_with_warblers_and_hawks.html.

... *blame its own St. Petersburg chapter*: "How State Bird Was Chosen Related by Mrs. Tippetts," *Evening Independent,* August 19, 1932.

... *spotted in thirty-nine counties*: *Multi-Species Recovery Plan for South Florida* (U.S. Fish and Wildlife Service, 1999), 260.

Motto: In God We Trust (All Others Pay Cash)

... *applauding Kimberly Daniels*: "Florida House Approves Bill to Post 'In God We Trust' in All Public Schools," *Tampa Bay Times,* http://www.tampabay.com/blogs/gradebook/2018/02/21/florida-house-approves-bill-to-post-in-god-we-trust-in-all-public-schools/; House Bill HB 839 (2018).

Nice workaround: Leslie Postal, "Schools Post State Seal to Comply with New 'In God We Trust,'" *Orlando Sentinel,* August 23, 2018; Cassidy Alexander, "Pine Ridge High Aids District in State Requirement to Put 'In God We Trust' in 'Conspicuous Place' in Buildings," *Daytona Beach News-Journal,* October 23, 2018.

... *did not meet with universal applause*: Robert M. Jarvis, "The History of Florida's State Flag," *Nova Law Review* 18, no. 2 (1994): 1050; Douglas, *Florida,* 158.

... *even a child could see*: Cory Schoute, "Class Project Leads to Bill for State Motto," *Sarasota Herald-Tribune,* March 20, 2006.

... *we're about a quarter of the population*: Michael Lipka and Claire Gecewicz, "More Americans Now Say They're Spiritual but Not Religious," Pew Research Center, September 6, 2017, http://www.pewresearch.org/fact-tank/2017/09/06/more-americans-now-say-theyre-spiritual-but-not-religious/.

Historian T. Frederick Davis: Davis, "Florida's Great Seal"; on Reconstruction see T. Frederick Davis, "The Disston Land Purchase," *Florida Historical Quarterly* 17, no. 3 (January 1939): 201.

. . . show less leg: UPI, "Florida Seals Its Fate—140 Years After Statehood," *Miami Herald*, May 22, 1985. See example: State Archives of Florida, Florida Memory, https://www.floridamemory.com/items/show/44002.

. . . the sabal palm: *Laws of Florida* Chapter 70–300.

Tired of lame jokes: "What Was Seal It with a Kiss?" *Orlando Sentinel*, December 21, 1986.

Firestone rolled it all out: "At Last, Seal Looks Like Florida," *Miami Herald*, May 22, 1985.

GEM: THE TALISMAN OF THE ANCIENT ENGINEERS

. . . was felt most forcefully in Brevard: Jerome Schnee, "The Economic Impacts of the U.S. Space Program," https://er.jsc.nasa.gov/seh/economics.html.

. . . space biz also overflowed: Faherty, *Florida's Space Coast*, 117.

. . . the layoffs had started: Ibid., 112; John Noble Wilford, "A Year After Moon Landing: Space Dream and Jobs Fade," *New York Times*, July 17, 1970.

"We're cheap, and we're proud of it": Charles B. Reed, "A State That's Proud to Be Cheap," *St. Petersburg Times*, November 2, 1997.

Selected Bibliography

Bartram, William, and Mark Van Doren. *The Travels of William Bartram*. New York: Dover, 1947.

Carse, James B., and James Foss. *Florida: Its Climate, Soil, Productions, and Agricultural Capabilities*. Washington, D.C.: Government Printing Office, 1882.

Cash, William T., and Dorothy Dodd. *Florida Becomes a State*. Tallahassee: Florida Centennial Commission, 1945.

Cox, Karen L. *Dixie's Daughters: The United Daughters of the Confederacy and the Preservation of Confederate Culture*. Gainesville: University Press of Florida, 2003.

Crist, Charlie, and Ellis Henican. *The Party's Over: How the Extreme Right Hijacked the GOP and I Became a Democrat*. New York, Dutton, 2014.

Date, S. V. *Jeb: America's Next Bush*. New York: Jeremy P. Tarcher–Putnam, 2007.

Davis, T. Frederick. "Florida's Great Seal: Its Historical Inaccuracies." *Florida Historical Quarterly*, vol. 3, no. 2 (October 1924): 16–19.

Douglas, Marjory Stoneman. *Florida: The Long Frontier*. New York: Harper and Row, 1967.

Du Bois, W.E.B. *The Souls of Black Folk*. 1903. New York: Oxford University Press, 2017.

Emerson, Ken. *Doo-dah!: Stephen Foster and the Rise of American Popular Culture*. New York: Simon and Schuster, 1997.

Ephron, Nora. *Heartburn*. New York: Vintage Books, 1996.

Faherty, William Barnaby. *Florida's Space Coast: The Impact of NASA on the Sunshine State*. Gainesville: University Press of Florida, 2002.

Federal Writers' Project. *The WPA Guide to Florida: The Federal Writers' Project Guide to 1930s Florida*. New York: Pantheon Books, 1984.

Florida State Library. *Florida Becomes a State*. Tallahassee: Florida Centennial Commission, 1945.

Gannon, Michael, ed. *New History of Florida*. Gainesville: University Press of Florida, 2012.

Gold, Pleasant Daniel. *History of Volusia County, Florida*. DeLand, Fla.: Painter Print Company, 1927.

Green, Paul. *Cross and Sword: A Symphonic Drama of the Spanish Settlement of Florida*. New York: S. French, 1966.

Kennedy, Stetson. *Grits and Grunts: Folkloric Key West*. Sarasota, Fla.: Pineapple Press, 2008.

Key West Woman's Club. *The Key West Cook Book*. New York: Farrar, Straus, 1949.

Lane, Mark. *Sandspurs: Notes from a Coastal Columnist*. Gainesville: University Press of Florida, 2008.

Mann, Florian. *The Story of Ponce de Leon: Soldier, Knight, Gentleman: Whose Quest for the Fountain of Youth in the Land of Bimini Led to the Discovery of Florida*. DeLand, Fla.: E. O. Painter and Company, 1903.

Martin, Sidney Walter. *Florida During the Territorial Days*. Athens: University of Georgia Press, 1944.

Morison, Samuel Eliot. *The European Discovery of America: The Southern Voyages A.D. 1492–1616*. New York: Oxford University Press, 1974.

Mormino, Gary R. *Land of Sunshine, State of Dreams: A Social History of Modern Florida*. Gainesville: University Press of Florida, 2005.

Morris, Allen Covington. *The Florida Handbook*. Tallahassee: Peninsular Publishing Company, 1969.

Moussalli, Stephanie D., "Florida's Frontier Constitution: The Statehood, Banking and Slavery Controversies." *Florida Historical Quarterly* 74, no. 4 (Spring 1996): 423–39.

Nelson, David J. *How the New Deal Built Florida Tourism: The Civilian Conservation Corps and State Parks.* Gainesville: University Press of Florida, 2019.

Roberts, Diane. *Dream State: Eight Generations of Swamp Lawyers, Conquistadors, Confederate Daughters, Banana Republicans, and Other Florida Wildlife.* Gainesville: University Press of Florida, 2006.

Pittman, Craig. *Manatee Insanity: Inside the War Over Florida's Most Famous Endangered Species.* Gainesville: University Press of Florida, 2010.

Stronge, William B. *The Sunshine Economy: An Economic History of Florida since the Civil War.* Gainesville: University Press of Florida, 2008.

Warren, Fuller, and Allen Covington Morris. *How to Win in Politics.* Tallahassee: Peninsular Publishing Company, 1949.

Watts, Frank C., and M. E. Collins. *Soils of Florida.* Madison, Wis.: Soil Science Society of America, 2008.

Watts, Frank, and Howard Yamataki. "History of Establishing a State Soil: Florida's Myakka Fine Sand." *Soil Survey Horizons* 31, no. 2 (Summer 1990): 23–60.

Wolfe, Tom. "One Giant Leap to Nowhere." *New York Times,* July 18, 2009.

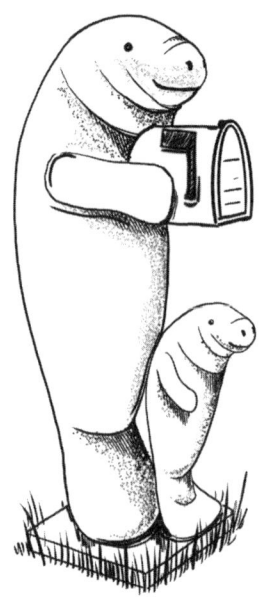

Mark Lane is a metro columnist for the *Daytona Beach News-Journal* and author of *Sandspurs: Notes from a Coastal Columnist*.